Scott,

The explosive growth of social media has introduced a new class of "influencers" on your business. Every day, tens of millions of individuals go online to broadcast their opinions, ideas and attitudes to the world on your brand. These new influencers control the conversation and play a significant role in shaping the opinions, attitudes and decisions of others. Smart companies are investing in deep market understanding with advanced social intelligence to manage their reputations, set strategy and drive decisions.

As a leading professional I thought your may benefit from this complementary copy of *Social Business Intelligence: Reducing Risk, Managing Brands & Driving Growth with Social Media.*

A collaboration of social intelligence experts in the academic and professional fields, this serves as executive handbook, exploring social business intelligence with analysis and case studies, providing recommendations about how your company can effectively implement an advanced social intelligence strategy, extracting deep insight from millions of blogs, social networks and forums to enhance your strategic decisions and drive your bottom-line and impact your overall business.

Sincerely,

Vincent J. Schiavone
Co-Founder, ListenLogic

info@ListenLogic.com | 215.283.6393 | ListenLogic.com | @ListenLogic

Social Business Intelligence

Reducing Risk, Managing Brands & Driving Growth
with Social Media

Stephen J. Andriole
Mark D. Langsfeld
Mark R. Harrington
Vincent J. Schiavone
Luis F. Stevens

© 2013 Ascendigm Press

Social Business Intelligence
Reducing Risk, Building Brands, Driving Growth with Social Media
First Edition, hardcover – published 2013
Ascendigm Press
ISBN: 978-0-9887311-0-3

10 9 8 7 6 5 4 3 2 1

Social Business Intelligence

Reducing Risk, Managing Brands & Driving Growth
with Social Media

Preface

This book looks at social business intelligence (SBI) – the mining of social media data that describes, explains and predicts multiple business activities. The intersection of traditional structured data (about customers, new products and sales) and unstructured social data (from Facebook, Twitter, YouTube, forums and blogs) represents opportunities for next generation business intelligence and predictive analytics. The billions of posts, tweets and blogs every month represent the richest communications and collaboration channel in history. Companies are developing their formal – and permanent – social media listening and analysis strategies as we speak. We offer some advice here, based on our experience collecting, classifying and analyzing social media data, and some suggestions about what your social media strategy should include.

We have been conducting social media research – and solving social listening/analyzing/engaging problems – for over five years. We published some of the earliest social media adoption data (in, for example, the December 2010 *Communications of the ACM*), and spent a lot of time researching what companies are doing with social media data and the full range of Web 2.0 tools. We have conducted multiple analyses on behalf of a wide-ranging set of clients whose problems crosscut multiple vertical industries, including retail, financial services, pharmaceuticals and entertainment. Each of us has been in the technology business for decades.

The book constitutes an assessment of social media with recommendations about how companies can implement social (media) business intelligence strategies. We offer a due diligence checklist for social media investments. Our case studies demonstrate the power of listening to – and analyzing – social media data. We also present opportunities for integrating unstructured data into business intelligence, conducting *real-time* social media listening/analysis and integrating social media into traditional (structured data) platforms such as customer relationship management (CRM), business intelligence (BI) and enterprise resource planning (ERP) applications.

Social media is another – richer and continuous – way for people to communicate, collaborate, share, search and transact. It has some unique characteristics and capabilities beyond what we've seen in more traditional "knowledge management" or collaborative applications. It's dangerous to ignore the internal and external potential of social media. Internally, there are numerous "social" applications that can contribute to operational excellence. Externally, there are even more problems that social media analysis can solve. There are opportunities to connect with customers and partners in ways that were impossible just five years ago.

In fact, there's no better connection than tapping into what consumers, partners, employees and even competitors think about you, your products and services, your company and your team: consumers have always had opinions; now they have public forums through which to publish those opinions.

The growing phenomenon of social media has resulted in a new generation of "influencers." Every day, tens of millions of consumers go online to express opinions, share ideas and publish media for the masses. Consumers control the conversation and play a significant role in shaping the purchasing decisions of others. Companies have to work harder to manage their reputations and engage consumers in this fluid medium. Businesses that learn to understand and mine consumer-generated content across blogs, social networks, and forums have the opportunity to leverage the insights from others, make strategic business decisions and drive their bottom-line. Social media monitoring is often the first step to adopting and integrating the social Web into business. There are plenty of monitoring tools in the marketplace that can give you data. But turning social media data into actionable social business intelligence is a different game. You need technology that's capable of collecting, filtering and structuring massive amounts of social data *in real-time*. While many social media listening companies claim to have such technology, very few actually do. We discuss here the capabilities companies need to optimize the use of social media data, to deliver true social business intelligence.

Whether you've just begun to develop your listening strategy or you're looking to upgrade your in-house technology and subject matter expertise, it's important to explore the options – and weigh the results – against your listening/analysis/engagement goals (which, ideally, are derived from an explicit social media strategy).

So given all this, what's social media really good for? How about the following – for starters:

- Market Research

- Brand Management

- Competitive Intelligence

- Product Innovation & Life Cycle Management

- Customer Service

- Threat Tracking

We look at each area and argue how it's *impossible* – in the early 21st century (and forever) – to ignore social media. The case studies in this book demonstrate how social business intelligence can inform business planning, strategy and decision-making.

So how can your company – any company – not leverage social media? How can any company not invest in a social media platform? While we spend billions of dollars every year on business intelligence (BI) – and billions (and billions) more on enterprise resource planning (ERP) – shouldn't we also spend some money on *social* business intelligence (SBI)? A more cost-effective investment you will not find.

Social Business Intelligence is a handbook for social media listening/analysis/engagement. It discusses the opportunities that social media provides as well as cases in social media listening/analysis/engagement that clearly demonstrate how the new channel can be leveraged. We also provide a long due diligence checklist for those interested in investing in social media. This "insider's" checklist is based on extensive experience collecting, filtering, structuring, integrating and analyzing social media data. We strongly suggest that you study this detailed list.

We also discuss where all this is going. Social media 2.0 is well underway and will not even remotely resemble what first-generation listening vendors provided to their clients. The "big data" problem will overwhelm most social media vendors as will increasingly specific business requirements. While "keyword" searches are "OK," they will not answer the very complex questions about customers, threats, brands, influencers or employees. While investments in social media will make perfect sense for many of you, it's also possible to ask the wrong questions, hire the wrong vendor and spend way too much money for too few results. Is this a revolution? Is SBI a disruptive technology? Will it persist as a formal channel? Easily. Social media is all of these things – and then some.

The book is organized in four parts. Part I positions SBI as part of an evolving "intelligence" journey that business executives, managers and analysts launched over a decade ago. Part II presents a set of actual cases that range across multiple vertical industries. Part III discusses SBI due diligence and SBI 2.0. Part IV closes the loop between SBI and BI.

We hope the time you spend here is well spent. If nothing else, you will gain an understanding of an exciting new approach to business problem-solving. But at the high end of your investment here there may be well be a game changing strategy.

Stephen J. Andriole
Mark D. Langsfeld
Mark R. Harrington
Vincent J. Schiavone
Luis F. Stevens

Social Business Intelligence

Reducing Risk, Managing Brands & Driving Growth
with Social Media

Acknowledgements

All books are team efforts. This one is no exception. First, there are analysts that look, listen and infer – day in and day out. They are a hearty bunch that seldom buckle under the social spigot that's on all the time. Erica Von Hoyer and Justin Melnick worked tirelessly to generate many of the cases discussed in the book. Their insights and analyses provide examples of just how diagnostic social business intelligence can be.

Without technology, there's no social business intelligence. The AKUDA LABS and ListenLogic technology teams that make collection, classification, analysis and reporting possible are – like the analysts who use their technology – the other half of the delivery team that enable social business intelligence. Our technologists have invented whole new ways to cost-effectively collect, classify and analyze big social data. We thank them for their creative work.

Finally, we'd like to thank George Nakhleh for his help getting this book into final form and ready for publication. Without this final push the book would still be "in the planning stages – but ready to go." George got it to the "finished" line.

Social Business Intelligence

Reducing Risk, Managing Brands & Driving Growth
with Social Media

Contents

Part I - Social Media into Social Business Intelligence

Chapter 1 - Social Media in Perspective
Chapter 2 - Social Business Intelligence

Part II - Cases in Social Business Intelligence

Chapter 3 - Apple
Chapter 4 - Diabetes
Chapter 5 - Luxury Automobiles (Lexus, Mercedes & BMW)
Chapter 6 - Automobiles for the 90% (Subaru, Mazda & Volkswagen)
Chapter 7 - Disney
Chapter 8 - Involved Viewers
Chapter 9 - Wisk

Part III - Social Business Intelligence Today & Tomorrow

Chapter 10 - Social Business Intelligence Due Diligence
Chapter 11 - Social Business Intelligence 2.0

Part IV - Business Intelligence Is Forever Social

Chapter 12 - Business Intelligence to Social Business Intelligence
Chapter 13 - Conclusions

Part I

Social Media into Social Business Intelligence

Chapter 1 - Social Media in Perspective

Social media is everywhere – all the time.

Wikipedia describes social media as:

"... media designed to be disseminated through social interaction, created using highly accessible and scalable publishing techniques. Social media uses Internet and web-based technologies to transform broadcast media monologues (one-to-many) into social media dialogues (many to many). It supports the democratization of knowledge and information, transforming people from content consumers into content producers. Businesses refer to social media as user-generated content (UGC) or consumer-generated media (CGM).

"Social media can take many different forms, including Internet forums, weblogs, social blogs, wikis, podcasts, pictures, video, rating and bookmarking. Technologies include: blogs, picture-sharing, vlogs, wall-postings, email, instant messaging, music-sharing, crowdsourcing, and voice over IP, to name a few.

"Social media have been modernized to reach consumers through the Internet. Social media have become appealing to big and small businesses. Credible brands are utilizing social media to reach customers and to build or maintain reputation. As social media continue to grow, the ability to reach more consumers globally has also increased.

"Twitter, for example has expanded its global reach to Japan, Indonesia, and Mexico, among others. This means that brands are now able to advertise in multiple languages and therefore reach a broader range of consumers. Social media have become the new "tool" for effective business marketing and sales. Popular networking sites including Myspace, Facebook and Twitter are most commonly used for socialization and connecting friends, relatives, and employees."

In many respects, social media is the natural extension of old communications artifacts like email, instant messaging, bulletin boards, chat and eRooms. It's also the end-result of pervasive computing, the "always on" phenomenon that became reality in the early 2000s.

Social media is about participation – by anyone. It reflects the democratization of computing, a movement that levels the computing and communications playing field. It's also fueled by "consumerization," where technology innovation and adoption is driven by requirements and preferences that originate with consumers (and consumer vendors) rather than cubicle-constrained professionals and their rigid corporate technology providers. (Today, new employees [especially Gen Y'ers] can be heard complaining about the inability to do things at work that they effortlessly do at home and on the road – everywhere but at the office. Not that many years ago, complaints went the other way.)

Social media is also about generational differences. Gen X and Y ("Millenials") are comfortable with technology (Gen X) and even excited about it (Gen Y): Millenials are, in fact, immersed in technology and assume IT. Gen Z, or "Zippies," don't even see technology as separate or unique. Those born after 2000 will challenge all of our ideas about technology adoption and optimization. Or, put another way, there'll be no need to study how quickly Zippies adopt technology or how well they use IT (information technology). IT will simply just be there the same way that chairs and toasters are there. *(Note the "official" dates for each era are as follows: 2000/2001-Present = Generation Z; 1980-2000 = Millennials or Generation Y; 1965-1979 = Generation X; 1946-1964 = Baby Boomers; 1925-1945 = Silent Generation; and 1900-1924 = G.I. Generation.)*

The key differences among the generations are behavioral – not technological. Millennials and obviously Zippies think nothing of sharing all sorts of personal information with their peers and even others in their spheres of communication and collaboration. In fact, definitions of "sharing," "personal" and "privacy" have all but converged: the younger you are the less offended you are about the semi-nude digital pictures taken – and posted for all to see – on Spring break.

Technology has enabled all this but make no mistake: social media is as much about behavioral changes as it is about always-on pervasive computing. The perfect storm of consumerization, technology capabilities and generational behavioral trends has delivered social media. Companies now must determine what they should do with social media. They have no choice. It's the new channel of the early 21st century. Social media represents one of the most profound changes – and opportunities – that we've ever seen in the way business works.

Social Media Drivers

What are the social media enabling technologies?

Let's start with the technology trends that enable all current business processes. Not so many years ago – as Figure 1 suggests – there was first generation (1G) automation and connectivity. We then moved to the early phases of systems integration and Internet connectivity. Pervasive computing came next, but the real excitement occurred when analytic computing emerged around 2005. Now we're in the "Enterprise 3.0" era

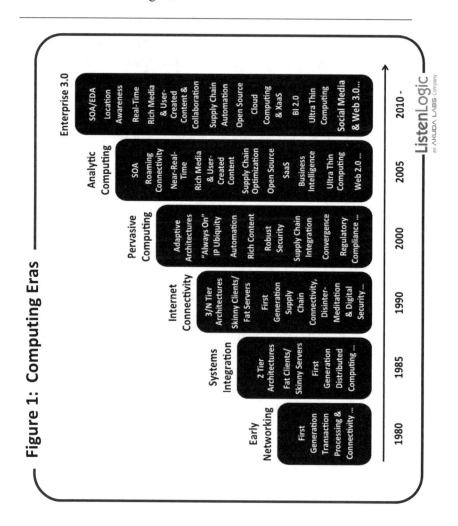

Figure 1: Computing Eras

The significance of the current era can be seen in the cumulative effect of the previous ones. Note that we're at a point where we're simultaneously integrated, interoperable, always-on, pervasive, analytical and converged. Figure 1 suggests that we've entered an era of business technology convergence. This means that all of the traditional lines we respected so much have blurred. Work and play share the same time and place. Organization and chaos live comfortably with each other. Privacy and sharing – with near-total strangers – has blurred. The current computing era explains a lot about social media. Computing and communications ubiquity is occurring in the Enterprise 3.0 era. Rich content is occurring in this era, as is roaming connectivity, full-view business intelligence (BI) and ultra-thin computing. Put another way, the sixth era launched our ability to continuously collaborate via small devices and rich personalized content, like pictures, videos and tweets.

Note that we're now in the era where computing is pervasive and fully mobile. The addition of "location aware" applications has changed everything: it's now possible to know where customers are, what they buy and even the behavioral cues that trigger purchases. Lead generation will never be the same. By and large, consumers will opt-in to the deals they receive by allowing their retail partners to know more and more about them – especially where they are.

We see the progressive eras as a march toward total mobility – a key social media driver. We also see Internet adoption and usage trends that surpass any previous technology in the history of technology adoption. We predict that bandwidth will be consumed at levels that dwarf the consumption of fossil fuels – which feels right, given how ridiculous our dependency on the energy past actually is. Bandwidth, transaction processing, interoperability and collaboration will all grow at unprecedented rates. Smart futures are always better.

Social media lives firmly within these trends. The intersection of behavioral changes, ready bandwidth, mobile devices and collaborative applications is fueling the growth of social media at rates that no one could have predicted three years ago. In fact, Facebook alone has become a small country. So has YouTube. By many accounts, Twitter is growing much faster than either of them; AT&T reports an almost 5,000% increase in mobile data traffic in three years.

But perhaps the most compelling trend is how content creation and content distribution are changing the way we communicate, collaborate and solve problems. The silos of the past are being replaced by business models that crosswalk old proprietary bastions of control. Apple, for example, blended iPods with iTunes as a new channel for the distribution of digital music. It's doing the same thing with software applications ("apps"), books and movies through the same distribution channel. Not only does this model channel tried-and-true software and content (and even service) vendors, it also empowers thousands of new software developers through a turn-key development/marketing/ distribution model that changes the way software is developed, sold and supported.

What all this has done for social media is incalculable. Not only has content creation and distribution changed forever, but the mobile platform has accelerated social media's adoption and penetration, since many of the standard applications for the iPhone and the iPad, for example, are social media applications like Facebook, LinkedIn and Twitter. Other mobile devices also enable social media. In fact, the particular device no longer matters: social media applications are as ubiquitous as the number of smart phones, laptops, tablets and desktops out there.

What about the "kids"? The discussion above about the generations and their predispositions toward technology is important, but there are other behavioral changes we should discuss. The whole notion of collaboration and sharing is fundamentally different today – and likely remain so forever – than it was a decade ago. The pace of this change is profound. Social psychologists and cultural anthropologists are studying the new behaviors and attitudes closely since they fly in the face of older notions of personal privacy. Notions of friendship, camaraderie and relationships are all changing. Inevitably these changes impact the workplace and attitudes toward individual performance and competition. Social media is both the cause and effect of these changes. Companies that initially banned social media from the workplace quickly realized that doing so alienated their younger employees who complained about their inability to engage in social networking during work hours and share the personal details of their personal and professional lives. These changes are permanent: it's unlikely that those born after 1990 will ever surrender their social media tools – tools that will be dramatically extended over the next decade.

So when all's said and done, social media is a behavioral and techno-logical phenomenon that originated with consumers but has now mi-grated to our professional worlds. Fun has evolved to work.

Social media is also a philosophy. While we still hear people saying things like "I'll never be on Facebook ... it's way too personal for me," Millenials and Zippies feel quite differently about what's "too person-al" and what's not. In fact, many of the questions Gen Xers might ask don't even resonate with their younger colleagues. The philosophical war is still underway but since the demographics are strongly with the youngest soldiers, the war's outcome is certain.

Social Media Applications

Wikipedia provides a list of social media applications (at this point in time). The number changes on an almost daily basis. The number of social media applications – and the creative use of user-created con-tent – is changing as our understanding of social media evolves and as our creativity about social media applications grows.

Examples (from Wikipedia in 2012) of social media applications in-clude:

Communication

- **Blogs:** *WordPress, Blogger, BlogHer, Drupal, ExpressionEngine, LiveJournal, Open Diary, TypePad, Vox, Xanga*

- **Microblogging:** *Dailybooth, FMyLife, Google Buzz, Identi.ca, Jaiku, Nasza-Klasa.pl, Plurk, Posterous, Qaiku, Tumblr*

- **Engagement Advertising & Monetization:** *SocialVibe*

- **Location-Based Social Networks:** *Facebook places, Foursquare, Geoloqi, Google Latitude, Gowalla, The Hotlist, Yelp, Inc.*

- **Events:** *Eventful, The Hotlist, Facebook, Upcoming, Yelp, Inc.*

- **Information Aggregators:** *Netvibes, Twine (website)*

- **Online Advocacy & Fundraising:** *Causes, Jumo, Kickstarter, IndieGoGo*

- **Social Networking:** *Facebook, Twitter, Pinterest, Instagram, Bebo, Chatter, Cyworld, Diaspora, Google+, Hi5, Hyves, IRC, LinkedIn, Mixi, MySpace, Netlog, Ning, Orkut, Plaxo, Tagged, Tuenti, XING, Yammer*

Collaboration/Authority Building

- **Collaboration:** *Central Desktop*

- **Content Management Systems:** *WordPress, Blogspot, E107 (CMS), Drupal, Joomla, Plone*

- **Diagramming & Visual Collaboration:** *Creately*

- **Document Managing & Editing Tools:** *Docs.com, Dropbox.com, Google Docs, Syncplicity*

- **Social Bookmarking (or Social Tagging):** *CiteULike, Delicious, Diigo, Google Reader, StumbleUpon, folkd, Zotero*

- **Social Media Gaming:** *Zynga, Empire Avenue*

- **Social Navigation:** *Trapster, Waze*

- **Social News:** *Digg, Stumble Upon, Chime.In* (formerly *Mixx*), *Newsvine, NowPublic, Reddit*

- **Research/Academic Collaboration:** *Mendeley, Zotero*

- **Wikis:** *PBworks, Wetpaint, Wikia, Wikidot, Wikimedia, Wikispaces, Wikinews*

Entertainment

- **Game Sharing:** *Zynga. Armor Games, Kongregate, Miniclip, Newgrounds*

- **Media & Entertainment Platforms:** *YouTube, MySpace, Cisco Eos, mtv.com*

- **Virtual Worlds:** *Second Life, Active Worlds, Forterra Systems, The Sims Online, World of Warcraft, RuneScape*

Multimedia

- **Livecasting:** *YouTube, Skype, Ustream, blip.tv, Justin.tv, Livestream, oovoo, OpenCU, Stickam*

- **Music & Audio Sharing:** *Pandora Radio, GrooveShark, Spotify, Guvera, Bandcamp, ccMixter, The Hype Machine, imeem, Last.fm, MySpace Music, ReverbNation.com, ShareTheMusic, Soundclick, SoundCloud, Turntable.fm, 8tracks.com*

- **Photography & Art Sharing:** *Instagram, Pinterest, Flickr, Picasa, deviantArt, Photobucket, SmugMug, Zooomr, Webshots*

- **Presentation Sharing:** *Prezi, scribd, SlideShare*

- **Video Sharing:** *YouTube, Qik, Vimeo, Dailymotion, Metacafe, Nico Nico Douga, Openfilm, sevenload, Viddler*

Reviews & Opinions

- **Business Reviews:** *Customer Lobby, Yelp, Inc.*

- **Community Q&A:** *ask.com, Askville, EHow, Quora, Stack Exchange, WikiAnswers, Yahoo! Answers*

- **Product Reviews:** *epinions.com, MouthShut.com, Yelp.com, Cnet.com, Amazon.com*

Many of these applications began as consumer toys. Many evolved into bona fide consumer applications. Now they're migrating into businesses of all kinds. This is "consumerization" – *and pragmatism* – at work. The evolution and direction of social media applications is important to understanding its potential – especially when software applications originate in fun/play mode versus work mode. The ability of "fun" applications to penetrate personal spaces is high – always has been – whereas the ability of "work" applications to penetrate "fun" ones is low – always has been. The assumption that one can find friends in real-time, for example, can – if properly nurtured – extend to assumptions about the location and preferences of customers. The sharing of information with friends of like-minds can extend to the sharing of information with employees, partners and, of course, customers. "Discussions," "arguments" and "negotiations" can also extend beyond the strict confines of personal networks. Applications like virtual reality-based simulations and really simple syndication (RSS) – among others – illustrate how intuitive extensions really are. Companies now proudly exist in Second Life (www.secondlife.com) and CRM processes now include social filters for their clients.

RSS filters are at work at the personal, group and corporate levels. Remember when manual search was all the rage? Now it's possible to tell a software application what you like, what your friends like and what your customers like, and task the application to go out and find the preferences and then report back to everyone automatically.

But perhaps the most important extension is "listening." Just as individuals want to know what their "friends" are saying about them, so too do companies need to know what their employees, partners, suppliers and customers are saying about them and their competitors. This can all be measured with social media listening and the "sentiment" that listening reveals. Suffice it to say here that the collection and interpretation of social media data can provide invaluable analyses and insight to companies who want to know what everyone says and thinks about them – and – most importantly – how that affects what they do.

This has always been the Holy Grail: *tell me what my customers really think about me and how – and why – they're likely to buy more or less of what I'm selling based on what they believe and how they feel.* Marketing and branding professionals take this data and re-craft their messages to consumers whose social media interactions profile their values, beliefs and attitudes about companies, products and services.

The above list of social media applications is a smorgasbord of applications waiting to go to work. The savvy social media strategist takes all of these applications and matches them to short- and longer-term business requirements. While many of them will fall right through the relevance cracks, some will rise to the top as hugely powerful processes and solutions to some difficult problems.

What should you do with all of these applications (and the data they generate)?

You need a strategy, an enterprise architecture, social media competencies and a social media project agenda.

A good social media strategy begins with business requirements and ends with the optimal matching of those requirements with alternative social media processes, behaviors and applications. The opportunity lies in the identification of the business processes, activities and models that might be cost-effectively enabled and improved by social media.

Lest there be any doubt about the pervasiveness of social media, note the following (from Wikipedia as of 2012):

- Social networking now accounts for 22% of all time spent online in the US

- A total of 234 million people age 13 and older in the U.S. used mobile devices in December 2009

- Twitter processed more than one billion tweets in December 2009 and averages almost 40 million tweets per day

- Over 25% of U.S. Internet page views occurred at one of the top social networking sites in December 2009, up from 13.8% a year before

- Australia has some of the highest social media usage in the world: in usage of Facebook, Australia ranks highest, with over nine million users spending almost nine hours per month on the site

- The number of social media users age 65 and older grew 100 percent throughout 2010, so that one in four people in that age group are now part of a social networking site

- As of May 2012 Facebook has 901 million users

- Social media has overtaken pornography as the # 1 activity on the Web

- In June 2011, it was reported that iPhone applications hit one billion in nine months, and Facebook added 100 million users in less than nine months

- If Facebook were a country it would be the world's third largest in terms of population, larger even than the US.

- In June 2011, it was also reported that U.S. Department of Education study revealed that online students outperformed those receiving face-to-face instruction

- YouTube is the second largest search engine in the world

- In four minutes and 26 seconds 100+ hours of video will be uploaded to YouTube

- One out of eight couples married in the U.S. last year met via social media according to statistics released June 2011

- One in six higher education students are enrolled in an online curriculum

- In November 2011, it was reported Indians spend more time on social media than on any other activity on the Internet

- According to a report by Nielsen, "In the U.S. alone, total minutes spent on social networking sites has increased 83 percent year-over-year: in fact, total minutes spent on Facebook increased nearly 700 percent year-over-year, growing from 1.7 billion minutes in April 2008 to 13.9 billion in April 2009, making it the # 1 social networking site for the month"

The Social Agenda

Just a few years ago many companies were trying to avoid deploying any internal social media applications. Some of them also avoided listening to what their customers and suppliers were saying. The turnaround has been astonishing: just about everyone has jumped on the social media bandwagon. Now the questions relate to ROI (return on investment) and TCO (total cost of ownership) – and, ultimately, the business value of social media. All social media strategies begin with business models and processes and end with a set of business objectives. The internal applications of social media must be specified with the same level of detail as the external ones. But before the matching between business models and processes and social media can occur, the models and processes must be defined and documented.

The ideal matching occurs when there's an existing model/process repository. Many traditional models and processes map well on to social media. Marketing, branding, product development, collaboration, innovation, location-aware processing, customer service, training and crisis management, among many other activities, can be enabled by social media. In some cases, social media applications represent alternative solutions but in others represent whole new solutions to some very old problems. Still another set provides similar functionality but for much lower cost.

Sometimes the potential of social media triggers the definition and documentation of business models and processes. Put another way, sometimes social media forces companies to think about the most productive use of the new technology through an assessment of the most likely impact areas. While this isn't the best way to proceed strategically, it may well take you where you need to go: matching business models and processes to social media for the express purpose of identifying high impact/low-cost/low-risk applications.

Ultimately, business technology strategies are about the optimization of business technology investments. Social media strategy is about the optimization of investments in social media. The internal and external strategies represent hypotheses about which social media technologies and applications will have the most impact on a set of business activities, processes and, ultimately, whole business models. It's important to develop this list and execute through a methodology that should include pilot applications, larger scale deployments and whole enterprise transformations.

Remember that the demographic that's hooked on social media will quickly become the demographic that spends serious money, runs companies, procreates and everything else life-long customers have been doing for centuries. Everyone needs a project plan here. The impact of social media will increase over time as it becomes increasingly mainstream. Traditional IT has to adapt to social media technology as it permeates internal and external corporate strategies, operations and processes.

For conservative strategists, social media is simply a new channel that – like the Internet in the mid-1990s – can be exploited. Ignoring the channel, as companies discovered the hard way regarding the Internet, will cost them money. Social media is continuous and real-time. It provides another dimension to BI. It represents new processes and even whole new business models for some industries. Social media also changes the way we think about very old processes and activities, such as surveying, innovation, product life cycle management, customer service and focus-group-based feedback. As the processes, models and technologies improve, even the most conservative companies will develop social media strategies.

More aggressive companies now have another filter through which to pass their business models, processes and objectives. Is social media as profound as eBusiness? Yes, because it represents an extension of eBusiness against a backdrop of collaboration and sharing on a real-time platform. Sure, a lot of the data is "noise," but strong social technology companies are increasingly able to separate the true signals from the noise and to interpret user sentiment, direction and likely behavior and – from good social signals – generate meaningful analytics.

Social Media Architecture

There are lots of decisions to be made about how to implement social media technology. For example, should you go with open source, Web-based applications or should you use proprietary applications such as those embedded within larger database and office productivity frameworks? Should you host the technology internally or should you rely on social media providers in the cloud?

Should you wait for upgrades to your proprietary applications that embed social media functionality or should you just jump to an on-demand delivery model now? (We discuss the sourcing of social business intelligence in detail in Chapter 10.)

An extremely important question relates to (big) database management. Data architects need to define the tools for storing, integrating and analyzing *structured and unstructured* data, information and knowledge. The storage issue is as challenging as the integration issue: social media creates massive amounts of data/information/knowledge that must be acquired, stored and analyzed. Are we back to the on-demand option? (Yes.)

Let's remember that social media is from many important perspectives a database management and analysis phenomenon – a very real "big data" problem. While much of social media "data" is unstructured, it's still index-able and search-able. Semantic processing is all about the intelligent parsing of unstructured data, information and knowledge. The challenge is the (fast) collection, filtering, classification, structuring, storage, analysis and application of social media data/information/knowledge to specific business problems and whole vertical industry domains. This ideally assumes the real-time integration of structured and unstructured data, information and knowledge.

Business intelligence lives where we analyze and solve. *Social* business intelligence lives there as well. The challenge is to collect and analyze social media data/information/knowledge from all possible sources and to interpret it in ways that are valuable. BI and SBI must be about business value.

Should you do all this yourself or should you hire a vendor that can "listen," integrate and analyze on your behalf? This question is no different from the larger database management activities at your company. Should you do social business intelligence internally or find help?

On-demand is growing dramatically. Should you partake? ([Again] yes.)

All of this sets the stage for multiple flavors of *real-time* mining and reporting – the Holy Grail. We've been working toward this goal for decades and now it's finally within reach. Multi-core/many-core hardware architectures can deliver the kind of performance we'll need to fully exploit voluminous real-time processing. This capability is well underway – and necessary for cost-effective SBI.

The architecture for social media technology is rapidly emerging and integrating with already significant technology trends in BI and predictive analytics. The emphasis will initially be on gathering social media data, but will quickly shift toward what we do with all of the data generated by social media applications. In other words, while it's useful to collect social media data it's far more useful to profile it, interpret it and make it actionable. For example, retailers need to know not only what their customers are saying about them *but what it means*. It's one thing to listen to social media chatter; it's something else entirely to listen to social media that informs the retailer (or HR professional) about what their customers (employees) think of them, their products and their services, and – most importantly – whether they're predisposed to buy more – or less – products and services from the retailer (or leave the company for cheaper/better pastures). The distinction is important: one set of data is static; the other is actionable. Similar to the distinction between semantic and syntactic processing, interpretive social media understands not just what customers are saying but what they actually mean.

Acquiring the expertise to fully exploit social media is challenging. Remember how hard it was in the 1990s to find professionals who knew how to build Web sites and grow eBusiness? We're at that point again. (And again and again – forever – as new technologies emerge.)

Social Media Competencies

While many companies have lots of professionals (and consultants) who talk a good social media game, the number of technologists that really understand social media is relatively small. This is especially the case regarding the integration of social media with existing enterprise technology such as database management, ERP, CRM, BI and network and systems management applications, and even more so regarding the exploitation of new hardware architectures. You will need social media strategists, architects and project managers. You will need hardware and software architects as well as specialists in database management, BI and predictive analytics, especially predictive modeling. You will also need expertise in Web 2.0 and Web 3.0 technologies, especially those that focus on text mining and semantic processing. Perhaps most importantly, you will need integration and interoperability skills that enable abstraction and synthesis: social media lives among – not apart from – all of the operational and strategic technologies you already have in your arsenal. You need professionals who can conceptualize – *and then operationalize* – how these technologies should work together to yield specific results. Architecture needs to be married to strategic planning, operational delivery and performance management. This is the team you will need to optimize social media technology for optimal business value – assuming you decide to build an internal team (versus finding a good social media partner).

You will also need expertise in social media vendor management since much of social media technology will live outside of your firewall in the cloud. Since many – if not all – social media services will be outsourced, vendor management experience with adaptive service level agreements (SLAs), performance metrics management, and related skills are necessary to exploit social media for BI and other purposes.

The necessary skills and competencies should be derived from your overall social media investment strategy. As always, good technology investments are the result of good strategic thinking. We should buy what we need. The social media skills and competencies necessary to exploit the new channel should link directly to the business goals your strategy defines, noting, of course, that strategies evolve over time. The skills and competencies you identify today may be expanded over time given changes in your corporate strategy. An example might help here. Assume that your company invests heavily in research and development (R&D) through an entire R&D infrastructure comprised of people, space, equipment, and a growing budget. What if a significant amount of that overhead was transferred to the Web? What if whole sets of R&D problems were outsourced via a crowdsourcing model? Companies change their R&D strategies all the time for a variety of business reasons. Social media crowdsourcing represents an alternative R&D model that many companies might consider over time. Significantly, we did not have the R&D crowdsourcing option five years ago. Now we do. What about product research? Can some – *a lot?* – of it be moved to the Web? There are numerous examples of old processes (and problems) that can be redefined through the creative application of social media technology. The skills and competencies around these changes should inform your human capital acquisition and retention strategies.

Chapter 2 - Social Business Intelligence

Social media represents an incredibly important opportunity to leverage new (and existing) technology on to internal and external strategic and operational business objectives of all shapes and sizes. Who, for example would have suspected that new product life cycles could be impacted by wikis, blogs, file sharing and opinions? That focus group in Peoria is forever gone, replaced by blogs, tweets and posts open to customers from San Paolo to Paris to Shanghai. Innovation is now a digital contact sport played by a globally distributed team. Customer service can be location-aware and real-time. Due diligence can be conducted remotely with bookmarks. You can track what customers, vendors, suppliers and partners really think about you whenever you want. All in all, you have the opportunity to engage in continuous conversations about everything that happens inside and outside of your company.

But you have to strategize properly. Like all of the technologies that have come before, you have to make sure that processes precede technology deployment, that you understand the technical and human resources necessary to exploit the technology and that you pilot the technology before you launch major implementations.

You should also appreciate the architectural sea change that social media represents. Arguably all of the technology that came before social media was "closed" and as such supported closed architectures and processes. Social media technology is "open," collaborative, scalable, ubiquitous and continuous. While security and privacy remain concerns, there's increasing attention being paid to security/ privacy issues by the largest technology vendors – who realize that their largest customers – conservative by nature – will need assurances that social media is "safe."

But the larger challenge is the new thinking required to exploit social media technology. While we love to use phrases like "sea change," "transformational technology," and even "killer apps," the fact is that social media is fundamentally different from traditional enterprise IT.

31

It's technically different and it's functionally different. It also alters business processes in some very unfamiliar ways. Who, for example, would have turned over chunks of the research R&D budget to Innocentive (www.innocentive.com) or NineSigma (www.ninesigma.com) five years ago?

The whole notion of crowdsourcing is anathema to the standards storm troopers of the 1980s and the device control police of the 1990s. The concept of asking employees to anonymously comment/vent on their companies' strategies, customer service and even leadership is not what they teach in business school. Replacing tried-and-true enterprise software applications with open-source social media applications just doesn't feel right to many technology managers. Content management through bookmarking and tagging? Training with wikis? Innovation with crowdsourcing? Recruiting with social networks? These are only a few of the opportunities that social media provide. Are there teams in your company whose job it is to identify these alternatives? Do they have the skills and competencies to do so?

The delivery of social media technologies also challenges technology acquisition, deployment and support models. Social media, while far from free, can be relatively inexpensive certainly when compared with the enterprise software licensing/implementation models of the past. It's also easier to deploy by increasingly technologically savvy business professionals who no longer need data center high priests to make technology work. Anyone can go to the Web and deploy social media technology – good and bad social media technology. This represents a threat and an opportunity. It threatens the control of IT but helps businesses think creatively about innovation, customer service, product life cycle management and countless other business processes. The acquisition, deployment and support of social media technology will necessarily be shared among internal and external technology providers – and by business and technology professionals. Everyone will need to widen and deepen their social media acquisition, deployment and measurement competencies.

Social Media @ Work

Do you know what your customers really think of you? Your products? Your brand? Your competitors? Your executives? Do you know what your employees are doing – and thinking – about you – *personally* – and the company, the industry? Is collaboration better or worse since you implemented an internal social network?

Social media is another way for people to communicate, collaborate, share, search and transact. It has some unique characteristics and capabilities beyond what we've seen in more traditional "knowledge management" or collaborative applications.

As you search for an effective listening/analysis/engagement platform, make sure that it provides the intelligence for identifying:

- Perceived & shared characteristics of your company & brand

- Perceived & shared characteristics of your competitors & their brands

- Opportunities to defend or build your organization's reputation

- Channels for revenue growth (venues, markets, influencers)

- Most effective methods & venues for engaging with consumers

- Potential threats to the company & company executives

- Trends for effective marketing strategies

- Innovation strategies ...

With an understanding of topics, themes, demographics, sentiment and trends, sources and influencers, enterprises have new opportunities for scaling business and protecting brands in an efficient and cost-effective manner.

To help you navigate the market, we've compiled a list of the key questions you should discuss with prospective vendors (we provide a more exhaustive set of due diligence criteria in Chapter 10):

Some Key Questions

- Are you looking for a monitoring tool or an intelligence solution? (Monitoring tools provide data, not answers: people are needed to interpret data and provide answers)

- Does the solution come with expert people that analyze social data and provide consumer insights... or do you need to hire and train them internally?

- Is data being converted into information and knowledge?

- Is the solution capable of segmenting based on department interests?

- Does it provide clear action items? Can it answer questions?

- Can the insights transform your business?

- How accurate is the data?

- How does the technology filter on phrases and remove irrelevant data?

- Does it use advanced natural language processing (NLP) such as "slop," "wildcards," punctuation, and compounded inclusions/exclusions rule commands?

- What is a benchmark percentage for signal accuracy?

- How accurate is the sentiment analysis?

- Does the system have the ability to refine and continuously learn sentiment?

- Is sentiment based on the brand and/or product, or generic sentence structure?

- How does the system apply analysis to punctuation?

- Is analysis based on sample data or all available data?

- What is a benchmark percentage for sentiment accuracy?

- How is influence measured and analyzed?

- How in-depth is the algorithm for making an influence assessment?

- Is influence determined on every post?

- Can posts be filtered by influence level?

- Can you drill down in real-time?

- Can you search within the data for "what if" scenarios or are the data filters predefined?

- Can you filter by any combination of keyword, topic, sentiment, demographics, influencers, sources, and/or time?

- After filtering, does the system provide full access to underlying raw data?

- Can it uncover opportunities and spot threats?

- Is it intelligent enough to detect the unknowns and ensure timely awareness?

- Can the solution be distributed throughout the organization?

- Does it have corporate, role-based dashboards?

- Is it easy to use or does it require specialized skills and training?

- Can the system collect/filter/classify/structure/analyze in real-time?

- What are the time intervals for aggregating, filtering, analyzing and indexing data?

- How long is the data stored?

- How long is data stored and searchable? (30 days, 6 months, a year?)

This list of questions suggests that not all listening vendors are created equal and that it's important to understand your listening requirements (from your social media strategy) before selecting a partner.

Social media is a moving target. What works today may be eclipsed by tomorrow's problems and capabilities. The larger questions are all about philosophy, predispositions, biases, demographics and measurable business value. There are executives today – still – that just don't like social media. (One of us can remember some years ago when a senior executive of a global insurance company declared in an all-hands off-site meeting that the "Internet was a fad that would be gone in a couple of years.") There are Luddites out there – even with the Internet, eBusiness and social media. Remember that just a couple of years ago lots of executives and managers banned social media. We're not exactly sure why, but even the attitudes among many technology professionals were often negative. But things have changed. Social media has assumed its place as a legitimate channel for a variety of purposes. It's impossible to ignore the channel if for no other reason than your competitors are working social media angles as hard as they can. Social media is new and evolving, but already contributing to the way companies conduct business.

What should your plan look like?

First, develop a strategy. Identify the activities, processes and functions that might benefit from social media. But remember that social media is a philosophy, a behavior and a technology. Philosophically, social media is about collaboration, sharing and continuous communication. Behaviorally, social media is driven by generations who've grown up digital, and technologically social media is about applications and platforms that are open, continuous and increasingly real-time. Many of them live outside the corporate firewall; many of them are moving to the cloud.

Adopting the social media "philosophy" may be your toughest challenge. You may encounter some Luddites that believe that social media's a fad that will be gone in a few years. There's not much you can do about this attitude if it's held by those in charge, except perhaps wait them out (or just leave the company for smarter pastures). They might change their minds, move on, die or retire. Behaviorally, the challenge is about openness, sharing, collaboration and, to some extent, anti-privacy. Technologically, social media requires a commitment to a technology architecture and delivery model that works for your company.

Your social media strategy should match business requirements with technology applications within the context of expected value. The business requirements should be defined around business processes and models that enable cost savings, revenue generation, improved service and/or regulatory compliance. The strategy should yield a slate of projects likely to achieve specific objectives.

You need to think carefully – and candidly – about the skills and competencies of your existing staff. Do they have enough social media knowledge and experience to develop your social media strategy, identify high-payoff/low-cost/low-risk projects, implement the project slate, measure the performance of all of these steps and adapt accordingly? This is a long list of skills and competencies. Is your team there? It's likely you have some skills/competencies gaps.

You also need to track social media trends. There will be new technologies (like Web 3.0's semantic processing and artificial intelligence [AI]-enabled automation) and new applications that re-define – again – key business processes and whole business models. The pace of change here is staggering. Tracking these trends and assessing their potential relative to your company's objectives is a new core competency. You absolutely need to understand, track, apply and measure social media. It's here to stay and will only grow as its champions age and are replaced by generations even more comfortable with the philosophy, behavior and technology of social media.

Let's look at several application areas in some detail. The six areas are defined around five questions, though the five by no means represent all of the questions social media can answer.

Market Research

What are the market research questions social media can answer?

Here's a sampling:

- What are the product & service trends in my industry?

- Where does my company stand in the marketplace?

- What does the competitive landscape look like?

- What are the major regulatory issues I face?

- What do people love/hate about my industry?

Brand & Marketing Intelligence

What are the brand and marketing intelligence questions social media can help answer?

Here's a sampling:

- What are they saying about our products & services?

- What products do they love/hate? Why?

- What are they saying about our company?

- Has sentiment changed over time?

- Why do customers buy from us?

Competitive Intelligence

What are the competitive intelligence questions social media can answer?

Here's a sampling:

- Who are our major and minor competitors?

- What are our customers saying about them?

- What are they saying about us?

- Who are we compared to?

- Who's number 1? Why?

Product Innovation & Life Cycle Management

What are the product innovation and life cycle management questions social media can answer?

Here's a sampling:

- Which new products have excited our customers?

- Which features work for them? Which do not?

- Which features should we introduce first?

- What new products do our customers want?

- Which do they hate?

Customer Service

What are the customer service questions social media can answer?

Here's a sampling:

- What do our customers like about our customer service?

- What services do they like the least?

- What are the "standard" complaints about our service?

- What are customer service "best practices"?

- What do people like most about our competitors customer service?

Threat Assessment

In the defense world, there's something called "Indications & Warnings" – "I&W" for short. Billions and billions of tax dollars are spent on I&W. The idea is simple: everyone wants to know what's going to happen, especially the bad things. So governments watch and worry. They use satellites, spies and even count the number of pizzas delivered late at night to their I&W counterparts (really).

So what about companies?

- What complaints are appearing over and over again?

- What are "Moms" threatening to do to us?

- What are the greatest threats we face?

- What will the government do next?

- What crises are likely to explode?

Social Media Strategy

There's no question that SBI is a priority. Without SBI how can anyone know what their customers think, who they like and who they hate? But there's much more to social media than meets the eye. Understanding the nature and trajectory of the social cloud is huge. It also enables additional primary and secondary business analyses. For example, the entertainment industry's social media intelligence might well focus on what people are saying about specific movies, television programs and radio spots. Tweets, posts and blog entries can add depth and color to commentary on various entertainment venues, but they can also provide additional insights into viewer/listener involvement and from that, infer which content is the most valuable to artists and advertisers, among other target groups. Social media can help correlate viewer/listener involvement with all sorts of activities through the gathering and analysis of social media intelligence. This kind of analysis can revolutionize the way we think about entertainment ratings, which will evolve from "what did you watch at 10PM" to "how involved were you in what you watched at 10PM" based on your participation in social media before, during and after your viewing of/listening to the content. Social media can also help design, test and deploy products and product enhancements. Why in the world would a company believe it absolutely knows what its customers want? Why not ask them? Why not try before you build – via social media?

Social media is tailor-made for innovation. Why not ask anyone and everyone about what's new? Open innovation is based on social media: ask and you shall receive.

How about competitive intelligence? Just listen to what they're saying about you and the competition. Listen to what they like and hate about you and your competitors? Listen to what they're saying about your competition's customer service?

The whole world of threat tracking and crisis management is huge. How many companies drive themselves into a ditch? Just about all of them at one time or another. How deep is the ditch? What's the best way to get out?

What about politics? What constituents say about their representatives – as sorry as most of them are – is of enormous value to politicians. Social media might actually become a communications channel that politicians can never turn off. It has already become a source of influence.

Last but not least, there are whole movements affected by social media. Who can deny the impact that social media's had on global political events like what we've seen in Egypt, Iran and Syria. It's positively amazing the power that Facebook and Twitter demonstrated in those countries. Are national and global referenda far behind?

Part II

Cases in Social Business Intelligence

Introduction to the Cases

The following case studies illustrate the power of social business intelligence (SBI). The cases clearly demonstrate the power – and value – of SBI across multiple vertical industries – reaffirming why all companies need social media. The industries we examine include:

- Consumer Electronics (Apple)

- Healthcare/Disease Management (Diabetes)

- Luxury Automobiles (BMW, Lexus & Mercedes)

- Automobiles for the 90% (Subaru, Mazda & Volkswagen)

- Entertainment (Disney)

- "Social" Television (Involved Viewers)

- Household Products (Wisk)

The first case is Apple and what the social conversation tells us about the Apple brand and then about the adoption of the iPhone 5. The two-part case is designed to illustrate just how pervasive the social conversation is (especially for large companies) and what one can learn from careful listening and analysis – especially around new product adoption.

The second case looks at Diabetes, the growing disease that will – according to estimates – eventually affect one in five human beings on the planet. What is everyone saying about Diabetes? What about treatments? Costs? Insurance?

The third case listens to what buyers of luxury automobiles think about their expensive cars, especially the servicing of the cars. Who's better? We look at Subaru/Mazda/Volkswagen in the fourth case to measure the perceptions, attitudes and sentiment of Subaru's customers.

The fifth case looks at Disney. What are people saying about what Disney offers – and represents? What do they "feel" about Disney? Why do they go to the theme parks? Again and again? We have the data.

The sixth case describes the Involved Viewer Rating (IVR) or the extent to which media mix and match within themselves. Do people talk during movies? Of course they do. But they also talk during *Dancing with the Stars*. We know what they're saying.

The last case compares results from traditional survey-based research to research based on social media. The case focuses on Wisk, the cleaning product that's been sold for years. The case compares and contrasts the results from each approach and demonstrates how insightful social business intelligence can be – and how limited traditional surveys really are.

All of the cases demonstrate the extraordinary insight that social media provides all kinds of companies that sell and service all sorts of things. The cases prove the extensibility of social business intelligence and the value of social analytics. But more importantly, the cases validate the social channel. Put another way, the cases demonstrate the risks of ignoring social media and the social business intelligence it enables.

Perhaps even more important are the engagement opportunities that SBI defines. For example, the Disney case describes "personas" that frequently tweet, blog and post about all things Disney. We know who these people are, what they say, and what they believe. Companies can engage them in all sorts of reinforcing – and perception changing – activities. Disney "Lifers" – one of the most significant personas – are potential Disney ambassadors who can be soft/hard incentivized by Disney to keep up their life's work.

Similarly, there are a lot of people unhappy with their luxury automobile experiences. BMW, Mercedes and Lexus need to know what they're angry about and how to make them happier. In extreme cases – especially if extreme patterns emerge – companies need to immediately reach out to disgruntled "clients" who've paid $50,000 - $75,000 for a car. They also need to understand what angers their clients the most (as well as what delights them). The point is that SBI is not just descriptive. It's also explanatory and prescriptive.

But what about the rest of us? Subaru, Mazda, and Volkswagen have social customers as well. What do they think about models and services? What the perceptions and issues around those brands? Who buys them? Why?

The Involved Viewers case is especially interesting – and valuable to those who buy and sell media. We know that those who watch *Dancing with the Stars* and other programs also tweet, blog and post during these shows (which are viewed when they air as well as anytime many viewers choose). The Involved Viewer Rating (IVR) calculates a combined score from social and broadcast media that reflects a new power score for commitment, passion, sentiment, interest, etc. – a score we never had prior to social media. This additional data proves to advertisers that there's more discussion about their products and services than they expected, and much more than the "reach" they get from traditional time-stamped broadcast media advertising. The additional insight translates into higher advertising fees for content providers since providers can empirically demonstrate that an advertiser's products and services are more broadly discussed than they were via traditional advertising.

The last case looks at what social media – and social business intelligence – brings to the traditional survey world. We look at the results of a survey around the cleaning product Wisk and compare them with what we learned from SBI. Yes, there's more insight generated from SBI than traditional – and extremely limited – survey research. This short case demonstrates the relative obsolescence of traditional survey-based research.

All of the cases demonstrate that social business intelligence (SBI) must become a core competency for companies that sell products and services to consumers. The social channel is ubiquitous and voluminous – and filled with data, information and knowledge about products, services, customers, suppliers and employees. The "social conversation" is 360, touching the entire product, service and customer life cycles. The ability to listen, analyze and engage the social conversation is as core as manufacturing, sales or marketing management.

Chapter 3 - Apple

Very few companies are as "popular" as Apple® (NASDAQ: AAPL). Many of Apple's customers absolutely love the company and its products. Some don't like the company. Predicting the features of new versions of old products is almost as exciting as predicting whole new product categories. There are those who wager heavily on features (as well as when new products will be released, etc.). Driven by a powerful consumer desire for its offerings, Apple has managed to disrupt traditional behaviors of consumers' technology purchases. Seasonal innovation within an ecosystem of offerings finds a saturated consumer market still lining up at Apple's doors.

How did Apple sustain such growth among a contract-locked preexisting mobile consumer base? Who was responsible for driving continued brand adoption? How did its reputation remain protected by consumers throughout a widely discussed labor controversy? SBI revealed answers to these questions – and more – that traditional research, analytics, and business intelligence (BI) could not provide. Apple's ability to generate significant dialogue among consumers and industry experts is an anomaly in the consumer technology sector. Marked by cult-like secrecy and a serious rumor mill, Apple makes its own the case for a comprehensive social business intelligence (SBI) program. Real-time intelligence is especially relevant considering Apple's widely anticipated "keynote" launches.

We know that Apple consumers and industry experts turn to social media to engage and express opinions, frequently revealing purchase intent. Traditional social listening, however, could not reveal the deep insight and predictive analytics that a recent comprehensive SBI program produced. For this case study, a 45-day end-to-end pilot SBI program was implemented. *Nearly 1.6 million individual pieces of social data were captured and used to inform a social landscape analysis, real-time analytics, and risk and reputation monitoring assessment.*

The answers to the key questions the analysis sought to answer were not only discovered through the "social landscape" analysis, *but they went undetected by industry.* This was a study that could – and should – have been conducted by key Apple management teams or Apple analysts. The findings revealed truths about consumers' perceptions of Apple's new CEO, the company's role in social responsibility initiatives, as well as areas depicting causes of perplexing growth and purchase patterns.

The results are summarized below:

Key Findings: Apple

Apple Conversations Increased in Volume by 35% from January to May 2012 (2,229,175 Conversations)

- iPhone volume increased 75% representing the greatest increase of the Apple product categories

- iPod references dropped in volume by 40% – the only category to drop in volume

- ≈ 100,000 posts include comparisons to competing brands

Positive References to Social Responsibility Jumped 79%

- Positive references increased from 6,800 in January to 12,200 in May

- The most commonly referenced social responsibility initiatives include:

- Addressing work conditions in China (5,100 posts)

- Efforts to reduce greenhouse gas emissions (4,200 posts)

Reputation for Producing Secure Technology Dropped by 25%

- Security is referenced in 4% of the total Apple volume (≈ 80,000 posts): recent malware issues and iCloud breaches have contributed to a *drop in positive references* from 9,600 in posts in January to 7,200 in May

ListenLogic
an AKUDA LABS Company

Key Findings: Apple (cont.)

Across Product Lines, *Peers* Now Serve as the Key Influencers During Decision-Making

- Peer Influence: across Product lines, Peers consistently represent high influence upon the decision to purchase an Apple product; Family has been displaced (as the key influencer), but is a close second to Peers

- Price/promotions has increased in influence from 12% in January to 20% in May; the influence is predominantly found in conversations where the consumer already owns an Apple product: in 5% of posts, consumers negatively respond to price drops, *indicating market saturation dilutes coolness*

Consumers' Interest in Apple HDTV Peaked in May (90,900 Conversations)

- Volume of references rose 46% between January and May

- > 50% reference rumored integration of Siri and Facetime

- 42% indicate an intention to purchase if/when it is released

iPhone dominates the Product-Related Conversation & Represents 27% of the Total Apple Volume (≈ 609,000 Conversations)

- Volume of references rose 75% between January and May

- Consumers discuss the newly announced contract-free option with Cricket (4% of iPhone volume)

- In ~ 6,000 posts (1% of the total iPhone discussion), consumers indicate that increased access drops the appeal (less exclusive)

- iPhone 5 is referenced in 59% of conversations (~ 360K posts)

ListenLogic
an AKUDA LABS Company

"Stand-outs" represent Apple consumers who like to have the latest technology and stand-out in a crowd; they describe themselves as being early adopters and typically have multiple generations of Apple products; profile has emerged in response to the iPhone product line with consumers in this group referencing frustration that "everyone has one."

Note that Apple has multiple "personas." The following figure provides the names and the breakdown. Apple has an enormous number of "brand addicts," consumers that just have to have the latest and greatest Apple products. Social media provides profiles of customers that exhibit certain characteristics.

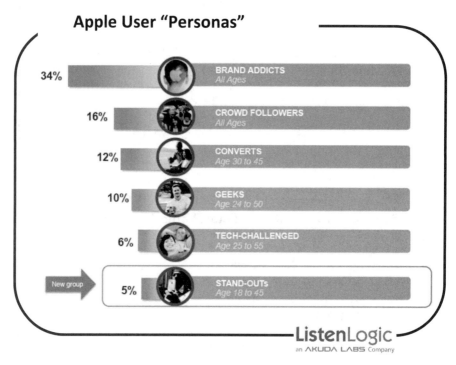

Uncovering insights about Apple required analysis that utilized a vast set of publicly available digital data that exists across the universe of social media. In traditional social listening, simple keywords are used to conduct search queries that usually sift a very limited data set. For this analysis, complex filters and concepts were developed to extend beyond traditional keyword analyses and data sets.

The analysis provided traditional and useful demographic segmentation, but it also revealed interesting and useful consumer behaviors observed across the Apple discussion universe. The segmented groups tell a very powerful story.

Of the ≈ 1.6 million posts analyzed, 84% fall within a behavior-based consumer group. Rather than use pre-determined user segmentation, our analysis revealed five groups that are specific to the Apple discussion universe. This specificity increases understanding and paints a better picture of users that is traditionally absent of segmentation methods. In addition, the consumer groups are extrapolated from a timely data set and reflect near real-time consumer actions.

The dominant group that emerged is "Brand Addicts." *These consumers represent 37% of the online user voice and appear across all age segments. More than half (52%) reveal a need to acquire products immediately.*

By volume alone, this demonstrates that the most vocal user segment is the one that is most likely to suggest an Apple product – a crucial insight that marketing should consider and incorporate into its media spend and messaging strategy. The insight gleaned becomes even deeper. *We see, for example, that Apple's Brand Addicts are responsible for introducing new consumers to the Apple eco-system.*

Financial analysts did not anticipate iPhone 4S sales to exceed certain levels. The primary reason for this prediction was based upon the fact that consumers were locked-in to wireless service term contracts, an upgrade barrier due to high costs associated with cancellation terms. They also believed that the iPhone was relatively saturated in the US and sales of iPhones in Europe were lagging their Android competitors. In spite of these guarded predictions, the iPhone 4S actually turned out to be the fastest-selling iPhone since the device's first version hit the market back in 2007. SBI revealed that Brand Addicts would circumvent the assumed contractual barrier-to-purchase by passing their current device onto a family member. This insight was available all along, earlier than traditional BI analytics – yet went ignored by the financial community and market forecasters.

SBI revealed an additional insight that financial analysts did not uncover regarding the strength of the Apple brand. The analysis uncovered how their desire for an iPad directly impacted consumer decision-making in other big-ticket and life-style financial matters – indicating quite clearly that Apple customers are willing to sacrifice to get an iPad (or other Apple products). The iPad comes with a hefty upfront investment unlike the iPhone, whose price is primarily subsidized by wireless carriers. *There is no surprise in discovering that high consumer demand exists for the iPad, but there is a big surprise in identifying how consumers intended to pay for one.*

The ability to uncover patterns and trends related to decision-making demonstrated that nearly 28,000 consumers planned to put off another purchase. Those sacrificed areas included other electronics, but the startling discovery pertained to bigger lifestyle events. *Some consumers planned to delay weddings, paying monthly bills, or even paying college tuition – just to get an iPad.*

Brand strength is a crucial factor in determining strategic planning and financial analyses. Apple's future in terms of its power to influence consumer transactions is obviously alive and well.

The fragmentation among today's consumer purchase channels is overwhelming for both consumers and marketers alike. For this very reason, it remains a top priority to understand how and when consumers are engaging and purchasing, and why. The present state of social media thought promotes a belief that word-of-mouth is king, and indeed it is in various instances among the social community. In order to understand this influence matrix, our analysis revealed levels of clear purchase influence.

Commonalities among user groups based on age, gender, and ethnicity were also revealed, as suggested in the following graphic:

Apple Demographic Trends

TOP THEMES by AGE GROUP

Age Range:	18-24	25-34	35-55	Over 55
Common Themes: (listed from high to low volume)	Product Line (28) Business Operations (20) Competing Brands (18)	Stock (29) Product Line (28) Business Operations (23)	Business Operations (36) Competing Brands (21) Stock (20)	Stock (29) Business Operations (25) Economy (17)
Volume %:	20%	29%	27%	24%

GENDER SOV

>55	51% / 49%
35-55	55% / 45%
25-34	55% / 45%
18-24	54% / 46%

Male / Female

Total Gender SOV: 46% / 54%

ETHNICITY SOV

White	Black	Asian	Latino	Indian	Other/Unknown
115	89	46	82	19	149

ListenLogic
an AKUDA LABS Company

Apple products are discussed most by those over the age of 55, but in a context outside of purchase intent. Consumers between the ages of 18 and 34 are observed to be the key segment driving intent revelations. Stopping here, it can be assumed that younger audiences therefore are responsible for first-time and repeat purchasing. Taking the analysis a level deeper, however, our analysis reveals behavioral nuances that provide a surprising insight. In the following figure, we see how consumers depict levels of influence via analysis of their historical accounts as well as their future intentions. We're provided with a clear picture of the differences in influence origin across four specific Apple product categories. Overall, family members and peers have the greatest influence on a consumer's decision to purchase an Apple product, followed by peers. This is most likely driven by consumers' need to experience products prior to purchase. Being able to interact with Apple devices in a real setting is more influential on purchase decisions than information offered by experts, interactions with sales staff, or marketing messages within social networks.

Influencer Findings: Apple

Influence Level by Product Group	iPod	iPhone	iPad	Mac
	n = 125	n = 125	n = 125	n = 125
Family 25%	HIGH 38	MEDIUM 25	HIGH 41	MEDIUM 21
Social Network 9%	LOW 3	MEDIUM 18	MEDIUM 18	LOW 5
Expert 7%	LOW 2	LOW 8	LOW 8	MEDIUM 15
Sales Rep 6%	LOW 4	MEDIUM 18	LOW 3	LOW 6
Peers 33%	HIGH 36	HIGH 41	HIGH 42	HIGH 48
Price/Promo 20%	HIGH 42	MEDIUM 15	MEDIUM 13	MEDIUM 30

INFLUENCER IMPACT on PURCHASE

ListenLogic
an AKUDA LABS Company

We have seen how SBI provides insight into areas of influence regarding Apple purchases, but the analysis also revealed information about what happens once a consumer becomes an Apple customer in need of support. An intriguing phenomenon was seen across the Apple ecosystem – peers are encouraged to consult each other first before embarrassing themselves by contacting Apple support.

48,000 peer-to-peer support discussions were identified during the analysis, of which 15% suggest that peer guidance should come before Apple support. The reason was not because Apple cannot provide adequate needs, but rather it satisfies the need to avoid embarrassment. It's better for Apple customers to feel like idiots among one another than among Apple's support experts.

Understanding key movements across social – especially for an online brand such as Apple – is a core requirement for any SBI program. Facebook, Twitter, blogs, forums, video sites, and image sites must all be monitored individually to understand where significant movements are taking place. Apple is a digital darling when it comes to online brands, so it's no surprise that the majority of volume around the Apple brand comes from Twitter, with Facebook a not-too-distant second.

For Apple, it's easy to understand when significant movements across social are likely to take place. Apple's keynote addresses, product launch dates, and busy rumor mill frequently drive volume changes among all the social media platforms. During this analysis, the channel analytics tool being used (see the next figure) alerted the analyst team of an alarm around increases across blogs and forums. The reason driving the volume differential turned out to be a potential major threat.

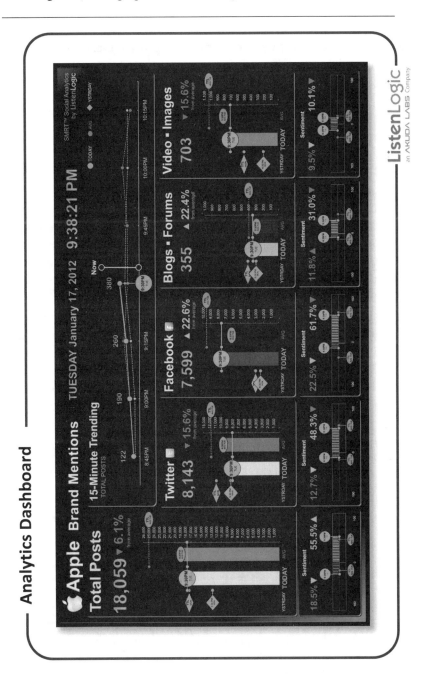

Earlier in 2012, NPR public radio journalist Mike Daisey produced a piece in which (Apple's manufacturing partner) Foxconn working conditions were depicted in a less-than-flattering manner – to put it mildly. Daisey and NPR later retracted the piece, with Daisey claiming that he let his theatrical approach to journalism get the best of him. The response to this incident – at all levels – was observed throughout its lifecycle during this analysis.

The results demonstrated that Apple was to emerge unscathed, with a segment of reactions depicting Apple as the victim of theatrical journalism. The issue of poor labor conditions was entirely averted. Had this story and retraction involved Microsoft or Google, the truth may not have mattered. The strength of the Apple brand was validated and there was no significant threat associated with the Daisey story.

The Apple brand is unique. Only the most robust social media listening/analysis companies can handle the torrent of conversations that are routinely pervasive. When Apple is about to launch a new product, the number and intensity of conversations increases dramatically. The iPhone 5 is a case in point. We listened intently for clues about the adoption of the new device – and discovered things that even Apple did not necessarily "know." The ListenLogic press release appears on the following pages:

APPLE'S NEXT FINANCIAL QUARTER WILL BE 'EPIC'

6 Million Consumer Social Conversations Reveal Strong, Rising iPhone5 Demand

San Jose, CA (August 2, 2012) – ListenLogic, a big data analytics company focused on understanding consumer behavior for large, corporate clients and consultancies, has turned its technology platform to answer a more broadly asked question: was Apple's (Nasdaq: AAPL) latest quarterly earnings report a signal to the market or just noise?

The company's most recent earnings were called "disappointing," causing a dip in the stock price and a rush for insight into the next quarter. For example, Piper Jaffray analyst Gene Munster found by asking 400 consumers that 65 percent said they expect their next phone to be an iPhone.

…

ListenLogic has built its own real-time, big data stream platform offering performance well beyond Hadoop and designed to provide market research, analytics and consumer behavioral insights to corporate clients. This ability to draw insights from massive amounts of enterprise and unstructured data allows companies to better manage risks across the enterprise and better engage customers.

"Apple is not a client, but many financial services and consumer products companies we work with are keenly interested in the company as a model. It is one of a set of brands for which we have created syndicated research offering deeper insights because of their role as essential markers for the overall health of the economy," said Schiavone.

In a just-concluded four-week period, ListenLogic analyzed six million social media conversations devoted to discussing consumer intent to purchase a smart phone. According to the company, the goal was to understand who the customers are, what they are buying and why they are buying. "Our mission is to discover answers to questions not yet asked," Schiavone said. "Our deeper understanding of big data enables this kind of real, predictive analysis."

In seeking an answer to the market questions about Apple, ListenLogic collected social data well beyond Facebook and Twitter, to include comments on news sites and forums, micro-blogs and online media, including video.

. . .

APPLE'S NEXT FINANCIAL QUARTER WILL BE 'EPIC' (cont.)

Among the findings:

- There was a substantial increase of nearly 50 percent in intent to purchase the iPhone5 as compared to data on the iPhone4S in 2011. Last year, 58 percent of the pertinent online conversations spoke to purchase. That number today is 73 percent.

- That 76 percent of the "intent-to-purchase" social conversations reference brand rather than any single, specific attribute of the iPhone5. "This intense brand loyalty is bad news for Apple's competitors who are seeking to either gain or expand a foothold," Schiavone said.

- Of the 17 percent who did reference a feature, screen size, a widely discussed "must have," ranked second with just over 5 percent overall. It was battery life (7 percent overall) that topped the list. Speed was third (5 percent overall). According to ListenLogic, there are no specific features driving market demand.

- Despite suggestions that current iPhone ownership and existing mobile service contracts might be a barrier to purchase, ListenLogic found that 82 percent who intend to purchase are current iPhone owners. Among current iPhone owners there was evidence of the emergence of both a personal and business device-specific ecosystem that will expand the market. Twenty-nine percent of those people who intend to purchase plan to hand their "old" phones and service contracts down to their kids, significant others, friends or within their business.

- The power of the Apple brand was seen clearly in the 23 percent of potential purchasers who said they would postpone buying clothes, cars, even booking vacations to make sure they can afford to purchase an iPhone 5.

. . .

APPLE'S NEXT FINANCIAL QUARTER WILL BE 'EPIC' (cont.)

- In a finding that could be interpreted as signs of strength beyond the next quarter, the number of consumers asking for recommendations for smart phones has tripled. Consumers intending to purchase the iPhone5 based on social recommend ations has increased from 48 percent to 82 percent year over year.

- *"This willingness to sacrifice to buy Apple products may be the single biggest measure of brand loyalty and the greatest source of anxiety for the competition," Schiavone said. "The current data show that only Apple can unseat Apple."*

ListenLogic
an AKUDA LABS Company

Chapter 4 - Diabetes

The Centers for Disease Control's (CDC's) National Diabetes Fact Sheet reports that 25.8 million Americans are affected by diabetes, representing a massive 8.3% of the population. 7 million (27%) of these cases are among undiagnosed patients. The report also cites that there are nearly 79 million pre-diabetics waiting in the wings.

The total expense of treating diabetic patients in the US has already cost $45 million to $120 million, and when we add indirect costs, such as disability and work loss, the figure approaches a whopping $175 billion.

Diabetes payers, providers and pharmaceutical and health services companies are constantly seeking ways to combat excessive waste. Traditional CRM (customer relationship management) and analytics solutions yield valuable data analysis to inform efficiency planning, but rising costs won't yield to even the best outputs. What is really happening after patients leave the doctor's office? How are caregivers responding to doctor's orders? The answers to these questions can potentially save billions of dollars.

The need for new solutions calls for a systematic, universal data analysis platform. Considering that 75% of US Internet users turn to the web for health-related information and advice, SBI is the natural response to this question of where to look for new solutions.

It's what SBI can provide the diabetes industry that is most exciting – the opportunity to go beyond a biased traditional research environment and learn about what patients, caregivers, and healthcare providers (HCPs) can't (or won't) tell you.

The best SBI research respects privacy concerns regarding digital social data. The rules of the Internet dictate that it is acceptable and expected in some cases to listen to what's being said, and craft responses and solutions to problems. In this particular case, the methodology clearly called for opening up the social gates and "listening" to key stakeholders speaking about diabetes online.

Over a 3-month period of time, social data was collected from among the online Diabetes discussion universe, a dataset comprised of posts made by patients, caregivers, and HCPs. *In total, an astounding 121,616 posts were captured across this spread of publicly viewable online diabetes conversation from the period January 1, 2012 through March 31, 2012.*

The findings presented here revealed answers to several key questions. First, consumers did indeed speak about what happened once they left their HCP. HCP interactions included those with varied practitioners, from primary care doctors to diabetes educators. Secondly, caregiver opinion and behavior was easily extracted and analyzed.

SBI is unique in that it never actually recruits respondents to participate in medical research. It uses observations of their *real unbiased* behaviors to extrapolate critical insights. It's also important to note that the data set utilized is representative of the offline population of diabetic industry stakeholders. The data behind the representative proportions are very large. The depth of the findings presented within the analysis was incredibly rich.

Several of the study's main findings are summarized on the following pages:

Key Findings: Diabetes

Diabetes Patients Discuss the Need to Find Medications that Allow Them to Maintain Accustomed Lifestyles & Turn to Other Patients for Advice Regarding How to Discuss This With Their HCP

- *Maintaining appropriate blood glucose levels is the primary concern for diabetes patients*; they seek to achieve ideal treatment without having to sacrifice enjoyable mealtimes and alcohol consumption

- Patients seek advice from other patients on how to best accommodate their desire to eat "anything" without having to mention this need to their diabetic treatment professionals, including primary care physicians, endocrinologists, nurses, and diabetes educators

- *Caregivers of juvenile diabetics are extremely active in the search to satisfy the "sweet tooth" needs of their loved ones*; they actively share recipes and ideas for sugar-free and diabetic-friendly sweet baked goods within diabetes-specific discussion spaces and general lifestyle blogs

Although Facebook & Twitter Host Nearly 62% of Volume, They Do Not Demonstrate a High Level of Influence on Decision-Making Regarding Treatment & Lifestyle Planning

- Facebook is primarily used by patients eager to notify "friends" of their successful condition management; though these posts rarely provide detailed information that supports development of a treatment portrait

- Facebook and Twitter are well-known status update vehicles within the social media universe and therefore do not spark in-depth engagement between patients and caregivers; replies to patient and caregiver posts made within Facebook and Twitter are typically met with congratulations and general support from non-diabetic affected users

- Fundraising and awareness posts dominate the overall microblog landscape, which is primarily the total sum of Facebook and Twitter posts

. . .

Key Findings: Diabetes (cont.)

Pregnancy Forum Discussions About Diabetes are Highlighted Throughout with Mentions of Hereditary Risks

- Mothers-to-be that are currently treated for gestational diabetes discuss the risks of passing diabetes on to their unborn children; members responding to these concerns direct these users to formal online sites so that they may discern the "truth" about hereditary issues pertaining to diabetes

- Pregnant women that mention being treated for Type 1 diabetes are not knowledgeable on the subject of hereditary factors; they are the most likely to tell others with like concerns to speak to their HCP for answers

Patients that Share Cost-Related Concerns are the Most Likely to Ask Their Doctor for Alternate Treatments

- Specifically, Januvia is cited as the most-difficult prescription to obtain due to insurance concerns; patients that discuss Januvia and associated costs frequently cite the need to speak with their treatment teams to develop an alternate course of action; strangely, they do not speak of bringing these concerns to their HCP's attention at the onset of being prescribed – most likely due to lack of knowledge regarding prescription coverage

- *Caregivers are more likely than patients to suggest prescription treatment plans;* they direct those with related inquiries to general prescription-saving clubs and sites, but do not demonstrate an overall knowledge about how these programs pertain to diabetic treatments

- Unlike other therapeutic areas (e.g., high cholesterol, high blood pressure, epilepsy), *diabetes patients base their knowledge of insurance coverage on co-morbid condition treatment; therefore, HCPs are most likely to be sought out as experts regarding which treatments satisfy insurance needs*

. . .

Key Findings: Diabetes (cont.)

Side Effects Do Not Impact the Treatment Decisions Made by Patients & Caregivers: The "Daily Diabetic Grind" is the Worst Part of Being a Diabetic, So Side Effects are the Least of Concerns

- Presumed side effects are not cited as a reason to deny starting a treatment; diabetes patients are "used to" daily scares and appear to be unaffected by (disclosed) potential side effects of prescription treatments

- Type 2, non-insulin dependent diabetics frequently demonstrate a belief that they will eventually need insulin and that their current effective treatments will fail; they cite hearing of others' experience and how these experiences are the expected course of their disease

- "Could-it-get-any-worse?" is the standard mentality demonstrated within discussions about selecting treatments; daily monitoring associated with the diabetic lifestyle is frequently cited as the worst part of being a diabetic – and "nothing-can-be-worse" hindrances to enjoying daily life, including potential side effects

Insurance & Costs

- Insurance companies are named in 1 out of every 8 insurance-based posts

- Co-pay mentions are generally informative, but a small segment of co-pay posts cite co-pays as being barriers to trial

- *Daily living expenses are a major concern; nearly 33% of these posts reference high costs associated with diabetic dieting needs*

- *Caregivers reference having to spend more money to feed "two" families - their diabetic loved one and the remaining members of the household*

. . .
an AKUDA LABS Company

Key Findings: Diabetes (cont.)

Treatments

- *Depression is the most widely discussed co-morbid condition currently being treated*

- Skin disorders are cited in 1 out of 6 posts about injection scarring

- Diabetic caregivers are not the main advocate for alternative treatments, and in fact tend to frown upon consulting treatments that are not conventional or suggested by a doctor

Insulin

- Insulin dependent discussions are primarily based upon exchanging experience with dosing schedules

- Convenience is a substantial influencer within discussions that suggest injection tips; Patients begin talking about injections and frequently begin tangent discussions about how they organize their supplies

- Humalog, NovoLog, and Lantus are triggers for discussions about fatigue, but not directly cited as being related to side effects

- Caregivers serve as advocates to the insulin dependent community regarding device reviews; they tend to share links to information about devices, both current and upcoming

- OmniPod and Freestyle are mentioned more within insulin-based discussions than they are in standalone medical supplies discussions

Medical Supplies

- Testing strips are mentioned more than any other treatment device; second to testing strip mentions is chatter about finding the right meter, and how it may be obtained
- Patients seek advice about insulin pumps regarding how to live comfortably with the device; they do not discuss choosing the right device or verifying the device that has already been obtained/used

. . .

Key Findings: Diabetes (cont.)

- Within syringe discussions, patients exchange ideas about preventing scarring; they frequently suggest specific lotions, creams, and home remedies to address rough scar tissue and site irritations

Lifestyle

- Diabetics discuss the inability to operate a vehicle and the impact this has on daily life and mobility

- Concerns mentioned most among the community include vision impairment, diabetic neuropathy, and weight control

- ≈ 220 posts within lifestyle discussions reference embarrassment over the need to perform diabetic treatment activities in public

- Patients are frustrated by employers' lack of knowledge regarding diabetes treatment; they are often upset over coworkers opinions that portray them as "gluttonous"

Diet & Nutrition

- Jenny Craig, NutriSystem, or WeightWatchers are mentioned in 8% of diet & nutrition posts

- Type 2 diabetics actively exchange ideas about how to "successfully" eat candy; these conversations take place primarily within condition-specific sites

- Low-carb dieting communities frequently host discussions declared for diabetics only; this phenomenon occurs across all low-carb related communities

- Caregivers discuss diabetic-friendly cooking options 3 times more than patients or other users; there is a very low presence of shared recipes that use artificial sweeteners

Fitness & Exercise

- Weight loss is mentioned as a key influencer for wanting to exercise; these posts typically occur immediately post-diagnosis

. . .

Key Findings: Diabetes (cont.)

- Type 1 patients typically discuss weight loss within "healthy eating" spaces (e.g., www.LowCarbFriends.com) while Type 2 patients primarily discuss weight loss within condition-specific sites

- Although low in total volume, a segment of insulin pump users "stylize" their treatment equipment to accommodate exercising; they purchase decorative bags and other personalized conveniences to make exercising "sportier"

Fundraising & Awareness

- Majority of "In Memoriam" posts due to viral Facebook "invisible awareness" post

- General awareness mentions that originate in microblogs are rarely shared or acknowledged by other users

- Fundraising posts are primarily made by affected members of the diabetic community; those raising funds share a close relationship with a diabetic, typically through a formal familial bond

- Condition-specific forums are not a significant source of fundraising & awareness posts

Experiencing Symptoms

- Discussion about testing & diagnostics is very high with majority of posts falling within the patient community; caregivers mention testing and diagnostics when referencing worry, fear, or other emotional discomforts related to thoughts about potentially receiving news of a diagnosis

- ≈ 35 posts reference *testing to "rule out" certain conditions* – of which diabetes and pre-diabetes are considered to be possible conditions

Assessing Risk

- Risk assessment is primarily made by patients who have been informed that they are pre-diabetic; hereditary concerns do not appear with high frequency at this stage

. . .

Key Findings: Diabetes (cont.)

Prevention

- Prevention is not discussed with high frequency at this stage; however, caregivers that engage in conversations with patients seeking risk advice will routinely provide tips on weight loss or healthy dieting

Receiving a Diagnosis

- Patients that post immediately after receiving a diagnosis mention regret for having bad habits; they immediately cite a need to lose weight

- Caregivers – especially children – are eager to determine their own risk of developing diabetes

- *Fear of diet changes is a routine worry at this stage; nearly 80% of patients that post at this stage (of which the majority are male) cite concern over having to make new eating choices*

Condition Management

- Switching conversations at this stage are typically related to what a patient has been suggested by a doctor; switching from one medication to another due to side effects is the primary reason for posting at this stage

- Patients that are successfully managing their condition suggest to peers that the counsel of a diabetes educator is crucial in order to "get used to" the diabetic lifestyle

SBI has the ability to capture and categorize data based on the actual user demographics – and beyond. In order to effectively separate user types, advanced SBI techniques were implemented. The powerful fact about our ability to segment audiences is that it does so automatically. This allowed for the analysis teams to focus on individual audience types separately rather than as a combined population. This requires advanced filtering methods that can effectively handle and run against large-scale data sets like the one collected here.

Broad user types – "personas" – were noted and included patients, caregivers, and HCPs. Traditional broad user types among the diabetes industry are not deep enough to reveal hidden insights. The analysis helped to uncover deeper behavioral groups, providing insight into the pain points, relationships, and needs – all critical decision moments – of organically identified groups. The following figure demonstrates the discovered online user types. Remember, these groups represent behavioral classification of users within an online base of more than 120,000 stakeholders.

Diabetes "Personas"

TREATMENT PRO *Age 18 and Over*
Discusses past and present treatments equally. Most likely to suggest treatment options to those seeking advice. Frequently shares links to resources.

FRUSTRATED YOUTH *Age 16 to 24*
Although small in volume, this segment is the most likely to stop medication at will due to annoyance. Participation is not ongoing as they seek specific advice in isolated incidents.

WELCOMING LISTENER *All ages*
Most influential segment regarding factual exchanges. This segment is comprised of patients and caregivers with deep knowledge regarding treatments.

NEWBIE *All ages*
Recently diagnosed loved one and desperate for advice. Mostly concerned with lifestyle issues and newfound restrictions, such as being unable to eat sweets. Seeks follow-up advice regarding HCP plans.

CONCERNED CAREGIVER *Age 25 and Over*
Mostly mothers of youth-to-adult children. Constantly seeking advice and feedback about treatments, especially regarding avoidance of side effects. Most likely to comment within multiple conversations.

ListenLogic
an AKUDA LABS Company

It's a panacea for those within any medical industry to – as a fly on the wall – see what patients are *really* doing, and not what they say they're doing. This is where one of SBI's greatest strengths trumps all other forms of traditional quantitative and qualitative primary research. The ability to observe conversations and isolated actions across a variety of varied public communities, without the presence of bias, continues to prove its worth and reliability.

Surprisingly, diabetes treatments are not the most-discussed topic. Certain sectors within the diabetes treatment industry should be interested in learning why this is the case. The story gets more interesting considering that the analysis manages to debunk a popular fear among pharmaceutical companies – that innumerable liabilities are waiting online preventing certain groups from harnessing the learning that can take place.

An overwhelming 22.9% of posts occur during the consultation and diagnosis phase of diabetic treatment. In other words, there are thousands of users within the patient and caregiver spaces that reveal what just happened when they interacted with a healthcare professional. It's interesting to note that these users are speaking more about costs and insurance more than any other topic. To have access to what patients and caregivers actually remembered experiencing, as well as insight into what they think and how they plan to implement next steps, is powerful.

To know what patients actually remember hearing is another significant benefit of conducting SBI research. The analysis revealed insights into patient recollections of interactions with primary doctors, endocrinologists, diabetes educators, and other field specialists. The recollections become extremely granular and reveal a patient vernacular that is specific to individual patient subsets. From these findings, patient vocabularies can be created and explored in further detail. During this analysis, a set of 22 specific acronyms and patient-centric diabetes terms were discovered.

In order to effectively discern when proper holistic care is implemented, social data can be overlaid with traditional sets of internal and external analytics. The resulting story can help define and address gaps and abnormalities that appear to go against data. Traditional data may reveal a high level of diabetic patient compliance with a high level of diabetics constantly reporting problems with controlling blood sugar. SBI can fill in the gaps, revealing where patients "forget" to share information at traditional medical touch points.

Chapter 5 - Luxury Automobiles (Lexus, BMW & Mercedes)

This case looks at consumer conversations referencing positive and negative experiences with Mercedes, BMW and Lexus. In order to achieve this deep analysis, ListenLogic conducted a custom social listening campaign focusing on a 12-month period from January 1, 2011 through December 31, 2011.

The analysis focused on conversations referencing a negative experience connected to the purchase or servicing of BMW, Mercedes and Lexus. Conversations included publicly-shared online content including but not limited to blogs, status updates, videos, photos, forum posts, review sites and comments to news media.

While conversations that occurred during 2011 may reference current or prior experiences, the analysis focused on the conversations that referenced an experience occurring within the targeted year. Also excluded (when identifiable), were conversations referencing a purchase from a source other than an authorized dealer.

So what is the volume and reach of the luxury automobile conversation?

Key Metrics: Luxury Automobiles

- 13,552,294 conversations referenced BMW dealerships and personnel (January 1, 2011 through December 31, 2011)

- 30% of the conversations about BMW, Mercedes and Lexus referred to personnel (7,600,293 of 25,536,559 conversations)

- 1,405,301 conversations referenced a negative experience with BMW personnel (which was 10% of the total BMW branded conversations; Mercedes negative w/personnel was also 10% of total; Lexus had only 5%)

ListenLogic
an AKUDA LABS Company

What else did we hear?

Key Findings: Luxury Automobiles

- BMW is the brand most often referenced in conjunction with luxury and success

- BMW: 14% (~ 1,950,000 of 13,552,294)

- Mercedes: 12% (~ 1,200,000 of 9,723,270)

- Lexus: 9% (~ 200,000 of 2,260,995)

- On average, *40% of the positive conversations include references to pampering treatment* (890,484 of 2,223,686): *15% of the positive conversations reference that the consistent experience keeps them coming back* (333,533 of 890,484)

- *53% of BMW's negative references cite that an employee's behavior is not what the consumer expected "as a luxury vehicle owner"* (30,693 of 57,429): when referencing that a negative behavior was not expected (as a luxury car consumer), 60% indicate that they have positive experience with another BMW dealer (20,089 of 30,693)

- BMW (13,552,294): Highest in volume of branded conversations: approximately 14% of the BMW conversations (~ 1,950,000) reference luxury and success

- Mercedes (9,723,270): Second in volume, approximately 12% of the Mercedes conversations (~ 1,200,000) reference luxury and success

- Lexus (2,260,995): Lowest in volume as compared to Mercedes and BMW, approximately 9% of the Lexus conversations (~ 200,000) reference luxury and success

- 79%: Specify an event or personnel trait that triggered a negative experience

. . .

Key Findings: Luxury Automobiles (cont)

Sample Verbatim:

"… was as nice as could be selling me the car. Once he got my down-payment, he actually started talking to another customer and left me waiting! I had to track him down to get an answers to my earlier questions" (Source: bimmerfest.com)

Sample Verbatim:

"… he treated me with disrespect, was condescending and downright rude. He seemed to decide I was a 'ditzy woman.' Little did he know that I'm the Sales Manager for a Fortune 200. Instead of hard-selling and bullying, he told me whether my offer was too far off and countered. Instead, he lost the sale. I drove down the road to Mercedes and couldn't be happier" (Source: community.breastcancer.org)

Sample Verbatim:

"Such an awful experience after they get you in the door. It's like once they have your money, you don't matter" (Source: yelp.com)

Behaviors Triggering Negative Experiences

- "Rude" (14,411): Consumer felt that they were treated harshly or unprofessionally by BMW personnel

- Condescending (11,631): The consumers felt that they were "talked down to" – that personnel was sarcastic or demonstrated judging behavior

- Inattentive (7,832): Consumers felt they were not receiving the full attention of personnel, that they were rushed, ignored or given the impression that the employee had 'something more important to do'

- Game-Playing (7,013): Consumers felt that the employee was not being straight-forward – had information they were holding back on or intentionally giving a run-around or 'act' that the consumer felt they could see through

. . .

Key Findings: Luxury Automobiles (cont)

- Intimidating (6,104): Employee bullied consumers by directly or indirectly suggesting that they know more than the consumer

Key Takeaways

- Consumers felt they bought a car and an experience; while they highly value 'pampering' (i.e. amenities, facilities, hand-holding), they most value a trustworthy and respectful relationship

- 15% of the conversations regarding positive experience with personnel include references to the convenience of doing business with a particular dealer – i.e., because they "trust" their rep, there's no hassle with future purchases or repairs; because they are "valued and respected," scheduling is easy and loaners are always accessible

The luxury automobile market is an interesting niche especially when one considers that the luxury automobiles are not – according to many rating schema (like JD Powers, which ranks [in 2012] Lexus #1, Mercedes #9 and BMW #10 in terms of initial quality [Mazda is #11]) – the "best" cars out there. Selling expensive products with questionable initial quality is always a challenge. Any and all information, insight and recommendations that help luxury auto makers sell more cars should be extremely valuable to specific dealers, brands and the entire luxury niche industry. There's also a real-time component to all this: when major problems occur, it's useful to know exactly when and where the problems are occurring. SBI can do all this – and more.

Chapter 6 - Automobiles for the 90% (Subaru, Mazda & Volkswagen)

While dreaming about buying – or actually driving – a luxury automobile is terrific fun, most people cannot afford a Lexus, Mercedes or a BMW. Subaru, Mazda and Volkswagen are brands for the 90%. But what do Subaru, Mazda and Volkswagen customers think about their cars? Their car-buying experiences?

Social data was collected from April 1, 2011 to May 9, 2011. Nearly 25,000 conversations were collected, classified and analyzed.

At the highest level, we discovered the following:

Key Findings: Suburu, Mazda, VW

- Brand Loyalty: in 16% of posts made by females, the consumer describes a specific model of VW or Mazda but "anything" Subaru

- Turn-offs: when describing why the consumer did not purchase a specific vehicle, the female consumer most commonly references sales experience

- Influence: females (30-45) most commonly reference that an online (special interest) community influenced her decision to purchase a Subaru; most commonly, community/babycenter.com, weightwatchers.com, and community.thebump.com

- Brand Advocates: the most vocal brand advocates are males under 29; in addition to positively promotion the brand, the age group represents the greatest ethnic diversity and breaks stereotypes

- When describing 'why' a specific car was purchased, the male consumer most commonly describes the driving experience

- When describing why a specific car was not purchased, the male consumer most commonly references price

. . .

81

Key Findings: Suburu, Mazda, VW (cont.)

- 22% of the male conversation references purchase intent; of these conversations, greater than 80% references an interest in 4+ makes of cars

- When describing 'why' a specific car was purchased, the female consumer most commonly describes the lifestyle-fit

- When describing why a specific car was not purchased, the female consumer most commonly references sales experience

- 80% of the female conversation relates to experience; 20% is purchase related

- When referencing purchasing intent, greater than 75% of the discussion references 3 makes of cars or less

- 23% of the conversations reference an interest and intent to purchase a Subaru (interest is short or long-term, may include a variety of makes and models and can include new, used or either option)

- Of the 23% of consumers indicating that they are considering purchasing a Subaru, 22% are open to options (both new and used are under consideration)

- Females 30-45 years of age represent the gender age group with highest volume of conversations followed closely by males 18-29 years old

- The WRX model is referenced within 30% of the Subaru conversations

- When describing how they initially became interested in a model, 16% of consumers indicate that they had a rental or loaner car that was a Subaru

- When discussing Subaru's models, 31% of the volume references more than one model within the conversation

- Subaru conversations typically fall under the following categories:

· · ·

Key Findings: Suburu, Mazda, VW (cont.)

- Auto-Specific Content: hosted by brands, brand advocates, auto-enthusiasts, … content is specifically designed to draw the auto consumer

- Special Interest: communities of consumers who share lifestyle interests, typically, related to the management of family, health and day to day life

- General Social Engagement: site is not theme-specific

- Males favor auto-specific sites for researching new purchases

- 63% of the purchase discussion volume is on auto-specific sites, 19% leverage special interest sites and 18%, social sites

- Females, while more diverse in their use of sites, favor special interest communities such as weight loss, healthy lifestyle, and hobbies for researching a new purchase

- 37% of purchase discussion volume is on special interest sites; 25% on auto-specific, 28%, Social

- When blogging about cars, men typically provide reviews of new models while females share experience regarding ownership

- Males favor auto-specific sites that target brands (Subaru and other makes)

- Females favor auto-specific sites that provide general consumer information (i.e. safety ratings, price, comparison tools)

- Of the variety of web sites, female consumers favor lifestyle and special interest sites for supporting their purchasing decisions; family and health communities represent the majority of the discussion

. . .

Key Findings: Suburu, Mazda, VW (cont.)

- For male consumers, special interest communities are fragmented (no clearly dominating site or topic.); while individual sites represent low overall volume of Subaru references, lifestyle 'themes' that most commonly include conversation are:

  - ➢ Health & Fitness

  - ➢ Local community

  - ➢ Technology – hardware/software, audio/visual, gaming

- YouTube content, primarily draws the male consumer interested in researching or discussing makes/models (68%)

- Speed is the most common theme of discussion (22%)

- Of the social networking sites referencing Subaru, Facebook ranks highest; most common themes include: owner experience (59%) followed by referral requests (21%)

Strengths & Weaknesses: Suburu, Mazda, VW

Strengths

- Brand portfolio ("I want 'anything' Subaru")

- Universal appeal – weekend warrior, hockey mom, adrenalin junky … praising power, AWD, comfort and space

- Popularity spans age groups

- High re-sell value and "last forever"

- Consumer brand-loyalty (especially with females)

- Reliability, low maintenance and fair cost of ownership

Strengths & Weaknesses: Suburu, Mazda, VW (cont.)

Young male enthusiasts – actively promote Subaru in auto forums

- "Community" – described as being part of the a club based on actual events but also, commonality of interests/bond

- Generational – parents buy for kids who then grow-up fond of the brand.

Weaknesses

- Subject of lifestyle stereotypes (lesbian, liberal and/or hippy)

- Males are not as loyal to brand – want to 'experience' other make and models

- Females < 29 don't view Subaru as being a 'cool' girl-car

- Inconsistent dealership experience – treatment by salesperson, repair costs higher than expected, multiple service visits required to fix a single issue, trade-in value lower than expected

- Mixed sentiment regarding gas consumption – across models, some consumers indicate a model is economical, others, that it is not

- Accessibility of parts

- Package options – basic is 'too basic' – add-ons require excessive wait-time.

ListenLogic
an AKUDA LABS Company

Demographic Findings: Suburu, Mazda, VW

18 – 29 Year Old Subaru Consumers (3,380 Conversations)

- 86% of the volume is represented by males and 14%, by females

- Of the 711 female posts, while sentiment is primarily positive, typically, the young female consumer describes it as a great car for her brother/father/ boyfriend

- Mix of ethnicities is highest within this age group – stereo type references are minimal

- Price sensitivity is high within this group – *approximately 70% of purchase-references indicate the purchase will be of a used vehicle*

- Planning a purchase for over 6 months is referenced in nearly 20% of posts; 312 conversations indicate that Subaru is their first car

- In 6% of the conversation, the consumer indicates that family members influenced the purchase decision

- 3% of Subaru owners indicate that they are in the military

Brand of Choice (Consumers Referencing Mazda and/or Volkswagen Alongside Subaru)

- Females rank Volkswagen as their first choice, Mazda second and Subaru third

- Describe Subaru as a family car; the brand is typically referenced within a Mazda of VW discussion with negative connotation (i.e. *"I want a new VW Beetle so bad but my parents will probably stick me with a Subaru"*)

- In 6% of the volume, males negatively reference VW stereotypes (indicating it's a 'girls car')

- Of African Americans in this age group (male or female), Mazda is the most commonly referenced brand of choice (over 50% of the African American conversation)

Demographic Findings: Suburu, Mazda, VW (cont.)

30 – 45 Year Old Subaru Consumers (5,798 Conversations)

- Females buying their first Subaru most commonly reference space, AWD and versatility as being factors in their decision

- Females most commonly reference that an online (special interest) community influenced her decision; most commonly, community.babycenter, weightwatchers and community.thebump

- Males most commonly indicate that their decision was influenced by an auto-specific online community; most commonly, a model-specific site i.e., NASIOC, subaruoutback.org and wrxtuners.com

- 17% of the volume is represented by males and females sharing survival stories (what they put their Subaru through); within approximately 26% of these posts, Subaru's safety/reliability reputation is referenced – most commonly, by females

- References to stereotypes is highest within this group: when describing themselves to others, male Subaru owners proudly indicate that they are "rednecks" in 98 posts (only 10 references are made outside this age group)

- 280 conversations negatively reference Subaru as a car for lesbians (219), liberals (110) and/or hippies (50); less than 50 references appear outside this age group

46+ Year Old Subaru Consumers (2,267 Conversations)

- The conversation themes by gender are similar in both nature and volume

- Across topics, sentiment is predominantly positive (little to no, negative themes)

- Affordability conversations typically reference a concern over gas prices: the 46+ year olds represent the age group most influenced by cost of ownership – in particular, gas (84 references) and service (73 references)

Demographic Findings: Suburu, Mazda, VW (cont.)

- Of 985 consumers identifying themselves as current Subaru owners in the market for a new car:

- 67% of females indicate that they would like to purchase another Subaru

- 8% indicate that their husband is trying to talk them into purchasing another brand

- 43% of males indicate that they are considering other brands – typically, based on an interest to diversify – not, in response to satisfaction

- In 220 conversations, females indicate that interaction with a salesperson played a factor on their purchase decision

Brand of Choice (Consumers Referencing Mazda and/or Volkswagen Alongside Subaru)

- Females most commonly reference an interest in having an AWD model

- In 16% of posts made by females, the consumer describes a specific model of VW or Mazda but "anything" Subaru

- Of consumer referencing that they favor Subaru over Mazda/VW, 78% live in rural communities; in nearly half of these posts, safety, reliability and/or cost of ownership ('will last forever') is referenced as being a factor

- Those in more urban areas, most commonly describe Volkswagen as their first choice; price is typically referenced as a reason ("good lease deal")

Commercials & Advertising

- Marketing is referenced in approximately 7% of the total Subaru brand conversations

Demographic Findings: Suburu, Mazda, VW (cont.)

- Positive sentiment exceeds 80% with females representing approximately 67% of the volume

- Males more commonly reference reviews, photos, or videos posted by other consumers

ListenLogic
an AKUDA LABS Company

The global automobile industry is enormous – and growing. But the process by which cars are sold and serviced is far from perfect. This in itself is interesting because of the amount of money involved in auto transactions and because of the obvious business sense of taking very good care of the customers that generate so much profit for the industry. But problems there are, and there's nothing quite like social conversations to locate, define and – if appropriate – address the problems. The ability to listen, collect, classify and analyze social data is the new best path to improved customer service and, by extension, process improvement and effective marketing. The two cases here – luxury and "standard" autos – demonstrated how vociferous customers are and how rich the conversation can be. The right social media vendor can make all of the necessary inference about gender, age, location, etc. – information that can be extremely valuable to auto dealers, manufacturers, industry analysts and customers.

Where does all this information reside? Where are the conversations occurring?

The following table presents the top sources of the Subaru/Mazda/Volkswagen social conversation.

Top Sources of the Subaru/Mazda/Volkswagen Social Conversation

Subaru	Mazda	Volkswagen
Twitter (S)	Twitter (S)	Twitter (S)
Facebook (S)	Facebook (S)	Facebook (S)
Clubwrx (A)	Forum.miata.net (A)	Thesamba (A)
Subaruforester.org (A)	Rx7club (A)	Passatworld (A)
Ultimatesubaru.org (A)	Forum.mazdaclub (A)	Forums.vwvortex (A)
Subaruoutback.org (A)	Rx8club (A)	Volkzone (A)
Blogs (collectively) (S)	Jlaforums (A)	Volkswagenvidz (A)
RS25 (A)	Mazdatruckin (A)	Clubtouareg (A)
Townhall-talk.edmunds (A)	Townhall-talk.edmunds (A)	Youtube (S)
Community.babycenter (L)	Focusfanatics (A)	Seatcupra.net (A)
Forums.evolutionm.net (A)	Blogs (collectively)(S)	Tumblr (S)
Forum.miata (A)	Mazdaforum (A)	Forums.bimmerforums (A)
Legacygt (A)	YouTube (S)	Myvwwanagon (A)
YouTube (S)	Forum.ea (L)	Blogs (collectively)(S)
i-club (A)	Mx6 (A)	Forums.fortitude
digg (S)	Community.babycenter (L)	Townhall-talk.edmunds (A)
Tumblr (S)	Forums.mazdaworld.org (A)	Volkswagenownersclub (A)
Forums.bimmerforums (A)	Mazdavidz (A)	Forums.pelicanparts(A)
Community.thebump (L)	Gencoupe (A)	Reddit (S)

(S) = General Social Engagement
(A) = Auto-Specific
(L) = Lifestyle/Special Interests

ListenLogic
an AKUDA LABS Company

Note the variety of sources. We discuss elsewhere in the book the need for multiple social data sources – and how only a few social media vendors have the capability to actually listen across the full social conversation. It's essential that your social media partner have the capability to listen to as many relevant sources as there are. Failure to listen broadly will dramatically distort the social message and the interpretation of the conversation. If you undertake a social listening project regarding automobiles or some other industry product or service, make sure that your listening partner is capable of comprehensive listening, collection, classification and analysis.

There's also a (generalizable) behavior continuum worth understanding. It includes three stages: those actively shopping, current owners and those generally commenting on brands and models – all as suggested in the next graphic.

Where consumers choose to have conversations differs – typically based on gender and/or subject matter, as suggested below.

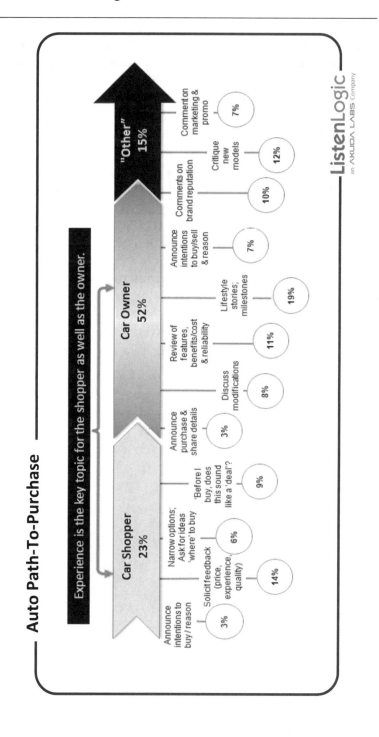

Men and women use the sites similarly though the primary difference between men and women is that *men make more of their purchasing decisions based on information in auto sites and women make more of their purchasing decisions in lifestyle sites.*

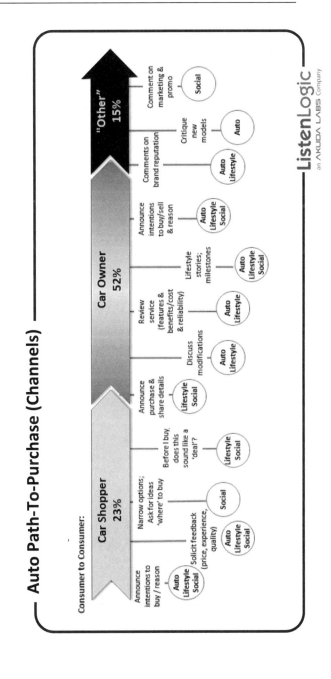

All of this illustrates just how wide and deep the social conversations are and how much data, information and knowledge the conversations contain. While the focus in this (and the previous) case is the automobile industry, know that the same richness occurs in the social conversations within many vertical industries.

Chapter 7 - Disney

Who hasn't been to Disneyland or Disneyworld? Who hasn't seen a Disney movie? The sheer pervasiveness of the Disney brand is one of the great marketing and entertainment stories of the 20th and 21st centuries. But what do people think about Disney? What do they like and dislike? Where are they likely to spend more – or less – money with Disney? The social data analyzed below was collected in May 2012 – just one month – when 4,830,676 conversations occurred.

Here's the high level summary:

Disney

- Brand image and reputation dominated the company themed conversations – 38% of posts

- Conspiracy theories, cover-ups, and political gaming were found in 9% of company related conversations

- *26% of the conversations were expense-related – ways to save money, budgeting, price increases, trade-offs*

What else did we learn?

Key Findings: Disney

Walt Disney is Referenced in 2% of the Total Disney Brand Conversation (≈ 79,800 Posts)

- 37% of references (29,500) include a Walt Disney quote or speculation regarding what he would think about a particular circumstance

- Within 14% of conversations (10,900 posts) regarding Walt, consumers share rumors regarding Walt, most commonly, an association with the 33° Freemasons (belief that Walt was an Illuminist who worked with government to program children)

. . .

Key Findings: Disney (cont.)

- 2% of conversations regarding Walt reference that Illuminists inspired the naming of Club 33° (1,800 posts)

Robert A. Iger is Referenced in 1% of the Total Disney Brand Conversation (≈ 32,800 Posts)

- 34% of conversations (11,000) compare Iger's performance with other Disney Executives

- 38% (4,200 posts) provide positive reference to Iger, indicating that he is forward-thinking and executes with confidence

- 16% of conversations (1,800) negatively reference his performance as CEO, indicating that he focuses on quantity (sales) over quality (experience)

- In 10% of conversations (1,100 posts), consumers positively reference Iger's participation on Apple's board and hope that it increases Disney's focus on innovation

Positive References to the Disney Brand

- 21% reference Disney "memories" with Disney Endings and Magical Moments typically playing a factor (> 1M posts)

- 13% of conversations (> 640,000 posts) reference Disney's responsiveness to consumers, Social Responsibility initiatives, and Sustainability efforts

- 15% (94,000 posts) indicate that Disney has inspired them to do good, typically, because they feel good: top three references are to wellness programs, youth activism and volunteering

- Of the consumer personas, "Lifers" (those who incorporate Disney into their daily lives) are most dominant – 20% of the volume

- 23% of Lifers indicate they became 'addicted' as adults

Key Findings: Disney (cont.)

6% of Conversations Include Activists Speaking Out *Against* Disney (301,000 Posts)

- Support of SOPA and CISPA

- Media control

- Animal safety and wellness

- Child safety

- Rise in prices 'to keep locals out'

- Characters encourage racism and sexism

- Copyrights (i.e. post acquisition of Marvel Comics)

- Despite being a negative target by adult activists, Disney is positively referenced for encouraging activism in youth (1% of the total Disney conversation ~ 64,000 posts)

Consumer Feedback – 3% of total Volume Questions Safety & Security (133,000 Posts)

- When seeking feedback from other consumers, consumers most commonly ask whether Disney can be trusted for safety & security; *within 41% of these conversations (55,000 posts), consumers indicate that they do not believe safety reports shared by Disney*

Discrimination

- 2% of Disney company posts reference discrimination (98,700); of these posts, 57% (56,500) are made in defense of Disney or against the consumers referencing discrimination on the part of Disney

. . . ListenLogic

an AKUDA LABS Company

Key Findings: Disney (cont.)

Good People & Good Lessons (≈ 480,000 references)

- 12% of Disney company posts reference the imaged portrayed by the Disney brand

- Within the image conversations, 17% reference Cast Member requirements (79,600); consumers share mixed sentiment regarding easing of requirements (sympathize with employees but fear long-term impact)

Can I Sue Disney? (≈ 195,800 References)

- 4% of the company-related conversations references lawsuits against Disney

- 30% of the posts reference allegations of mistreatment by Cast Members or injuries due to negligence on the part of Disney (58,700)

- *19% of the posts reference a form of discrimination – race, looks, religion, weight, impairments, sexual orientation (36,200)*

ListenLogic

an AKUDA LABS Company

Disney – like all major companies that interact with consumers – has "personas" that comment frequently on the Disney experience. The figure below presents the six personas that dominate the Disney social conversation. Lifers, Believers and Experiencers are passionate about their Disney experiences.

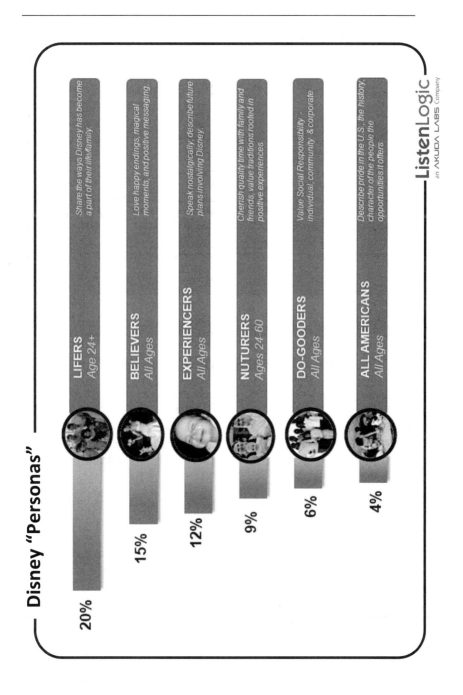

Disney "Personas"

LIFERS Age 24+ — Share the ways Disney has become a part of their life/family. — 20%

BELIEVERS All Ages — Love happy endings, magical moments, and positive messaging. — 15%

EXPERIENCERS All Ages — Speak nostalgically, describe future plans involving Disney. — 12%

NUTURERS Ages 24-60 — Cherish quality time with family and friends, value traditions rooted in positive experiences — 9%

DO-GOODERS All Ages — Value Social Responsibility - individual, community & corporate. — 6%

ALL AMERICANS All Ages — Describe pride in the U.S. the history, character of the people the opportunities it offers — 4%

ListenLogic an AKUDA LABS Company

"Persona" Insights: Disney

23% of "Lifers" Became "Addicted to Disney" As An Adult

- "Lifers" represent consumers who indicate they 'can't get enough' of Disney; they typically describe the 'experience' and 'magic' of Disney and share the ways they cultivate these experiences – sharing with like-minded individuals, scrapbooking, viewing Disney programs, using advanced planning for trips as a way to motivate or incentivize family members and self (weight-loss, curb spending, quit smoking, improve overall health)

  ➢ 23% indicate that their for passion for Disney began in adulthood (231 of 1,011)

  ➢ 34% (89 of 231) in response to experience of family members

  ➢ 24% (55 of 231) indicate it began in response to a honeymoon

  ➢ 15% (31 of 231) following an interest for a movie or show

Lifers

- Share their experiences across a variety of online networks; provide travel and savings tips, maintain a blog or participate in a forum with posts providing planning for future trip, details of past trip(s), or comparison of experiences; dream of joining Club 33°

- Discuss gift giving for family members; describe their personal wish list items needed to complete collections

- Indicate that they value programming because it is a dependable source for positive messaging; relate storylines to "real life"

- Defend Disney when negative comments from others; indicate that Disney leads by example

ListenLogic
an AKUDA LABS Company

The demographic data extracted from tweets, blogs and posts was also revealing as suggested by the following graphic. Note the distribution of age groups, the common themes and the volume. Gender and race/ethnicity is also segmented. The figure illustrates the importance of segmentation, but does little to describe exactly how age/race/ethnicity/location/income/etc. segmentation occurs.

Similar to the requirement to comprehensively collect as many sources of social data as possible, social media listening vendors should also be able to infer and extrapolate from social media data, information and knowledge. The following figure illustrates the results of technology capable of collecting, classifying, segmenting and analyzing mountains of social media data.

Demographic Trends: Disney

TOP THEMES by AGE GROUP

Age Range:	18-24	25-34	35-55	Over 55
Common Themes: (listed from high to low volume)	Brand Reputation (28) Experience (20) Planning (18)	Experience (29) Brand Reputation (28) Planning (23)	Planning (36) Brand Reputation (21) Tips & Tricks (20)	Experience (29) Tips & Tricks (25) Brand Reputation (17)
Volume %:	19%	28%	31%	22%

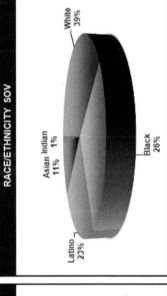

RACE/ETHNICITY SOV

White 39%
Black 26%
Latino 23%
Asian Indian 11%
Indian 1%

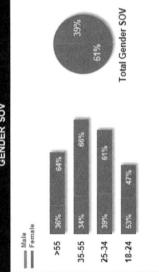

GENDER SOV

Male / Female

	Male	Female
>55	36%	64%
35-55	34%	66%
25-34	39%	61%
18-24	53%	47%

Total Gender SOV: 61% / 39%

ListenLogic
an AKUDA LABS Company

The volume of Business Operations posts increased primarily in response to the analysis of management activity and safety and security concerns. Consumers question whether Disney is forthcoming regarding incidents. While Disney is positively referenced with regard to social responsibility, the volume increase is primarily attributed to comparisons with other businesses (Disney is 'great' and better than the other Fortune-ranked businesses). Disney's control of media is negatively described in 10% of posts.

What about value?

Value Perception: Disney

21% of the Disney Company Conversations Reference Return on Investment (704,600 Posts)

- 64% Consumers share that they are not disappointed in the amount of money that they have spent with/on Disney (260,100)

- *37% indicate concern regarding price increases but a willingness to find a way to save accordingly*

- 25% describe research and innovation as being key to company profits (177,900)

How about the "face" and "voice" of Disney?

"Face" and "Voice" of Disney

The Face of Disney

- Sympathize with Cast Members

- Indicate an interest in becoming involved (volunteer or paid) in order to have access to insider information

- Speculate what information is made available to Cast Members

. . .

"Face" and "Voice" of Disney

- Applaud Cast Members' ability to remain positive regardless of conditions

The Voice of Disney

- Website tools and ease of use

- Responsiveness of online Cast Members

- Posts by celebrities

- Believe that Disney Cast Members post to forums as consumers (1,800 of 3,000 negative posts)

Chapter 8 - Involved Viewers

One of the amazing aspects of social media and the social business intelligence it enables is the derivative properties of the social conversation. Not only do people tweet, blog and post all the time, but they do so while engaging in other very different activities.

What does this mean?

When people attend movies and concerts, watch TV and listen to various flavors of audio, they also tweet, blog and post. When they attend classes, eat at restaurants and shop in stores or offline, they tweet, blog and post. When they read books, eat dinner at home and play with their kids, they tweet, blog and post.

We've developed a quantitative metric that measures the extent to which viewers are simultaneously involved in multiple activities. This means that we can listen to people watching.

Our methodology is applied in this case to listening to people watching television. The methodology begins with the identification of consumer conversations by applying phrase detection (wildcards, identifiers), and inclusionary concepts consistently across each program to address the challenges of "House," "Community," "Parenthood" among others, as well as exclusionary concepts for each TV show to address background noise. The consumer conversations are then quantified during the 24-hour period after the airing of specific TV shows, and then normalized by the daily average discussion (excluding the show airing date). Conversations are then correlated to audience size to generate the index. Sentiment is calculated by positive % - negative %. A more detailed description of the methodology appears below:

VER™ Methodology

- **Involved Viewer Rating™ (VER™)**: Viewer involvement in the show relative to its audience size

- The metric is quantified by:

Online Conversations (subset)

$$\frac{\text{Online Conversations (subset)}}{\text{Audience Size}} \times constant = \text{VER Index}$$

- **Viewer Opinion Rating™ (VOR™)**: Total positive/negative opinion of the show

- **Show Insights**: Qualitative and quantitative insights extrapolating top themes, demographics and trending

We use multi-dimensional (vector-based) and statistical Bayes analysis to segment consumers by age, gender and ethnicity. Our 50-factor algorithm with machine-learning technology processes:

- Language (phrases used)

- Imagery (facial matching from profiles)

- Interests and Hobbies (profile data)

- Names (first name, last name)

So the question is: are audience viewership and online conversations correlated?

The following charts illustrate just how powerfully viewership and social conversations correlate. The charts also illustrate that the correlations can be deadly – and counter-intuitive.

Why deadly and counter-intuitive?

The "perfect" TV show is ranked #1 in viewership and #1 in posts, tweets and blogs. The first chart on *Dancing with the Stars* suggests patterns regarding online "participation" in the programming, with activities building toward the show's finale. The next chart looks at *The Daily Show*.

The charts correlate activity over a short period of time (from 9/24/10 through 11/29/10). They first reveal the new media reality – the co-occurrence of experiences. They also reveal the relative status of each media: while TV viewership has been important to advertisers for decades, we now have a new "channel" – social media – which is quickly becoming just as important – and the basis for higher (and lower) advertising fees. From this point on media will be simultaneously mixed, measured and priced. While three years ago it might have been possible to ignore social data, information and knowledge, today (and going forward forever) it's impossible to ignore the social conversation.

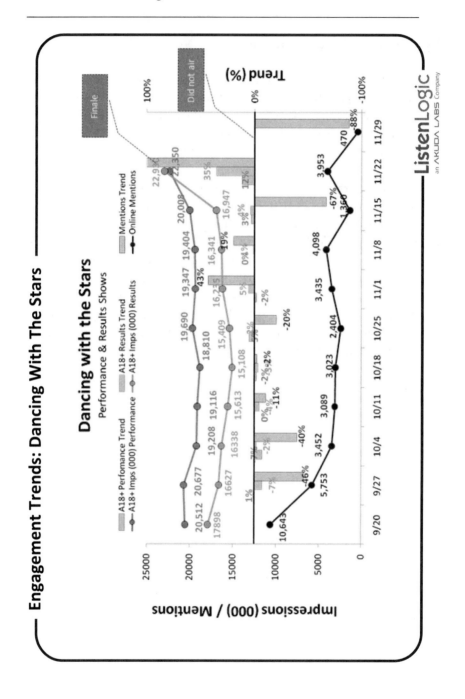

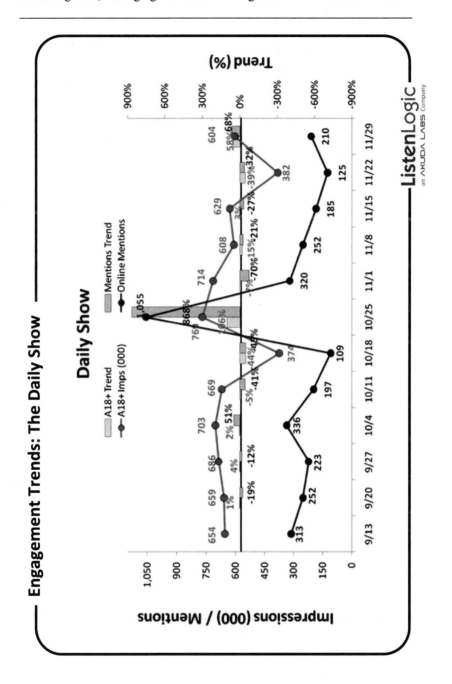

The following table reveals the essence of the correlations. Note the long list of TV shows and IVR scores. The contrasts are positively striking. Note how many programs have huge viewership/IVR variance. *Sons of Anarchy* has a high IVR rank but low viewership, while *The Mentalist* has high viewership but an extremely low IVR. Shows like *Dancing with the Stars* on the other hand have both: high viewership and high IVR.

The figures also display the variances between the two metrics.

Viewership & IVR Variance

PROGRAM	NETWORK	AUDIENCE RANK	IVR RANK	DAY
SONS OF ANARCHY	FX	39	1	Tuesday
GLEE	FOX	22	2	Tuesday
STORM CHASERS	DIS	49	3	Wednesday
HOARDERS	A&E	40	4	Monday
DAILY SHOW	CC	46	5	mon-thurs
TOP CHEF	BRAVO	54	6	Wednesday
IRON CHEF AMERICA	FN	48	7	Sunday
DANCING WITH THE STARS	ABC	1	8	Monday
IT'S ALWAYS SUNNY IN PHILADELPHIA	FX	45	9	Thursday
DANCING WITH THE STARS	ABC	3	10	Tuesday
PRIVATE PRACTICE	ABC	16	11	Thursday
THE SIMPSONS	FOX	26	12	Sunday
DIRTY JOBS	DIS	51	13	Tuesday
PAWN STARS	HIS	38	14	Monday
COMMUNITY	NBC	34	15	Thursday
THE BIGGEST LOSER	NBC	25	16	Tuesday
CHUCK	NBC	31	17	Monday
HOUSE	FOX	36	18	Monday
HOUSE OF PAYNE	TBS	52	19	Wednesday
THE NEXT IRON CHEF AMERICA	FN	43	20	Sunday
30 ROCK	NBC	29	21	Thursday
THE AMAZING RACE	CBS	17	22	Sunday
THE OFFICE	NBC	20	23	Thursday
THE APPRENTICE	NBC	35	24	Thursday
UNDERCOVERS	NBC	30	25	Wednesday
GREY'S ANATOMY	ABC	10	26	Thursday
CRIMINAL MINDS	CBS	4	27	Wednesday
DESPERATE HOUSEWIVES	ABC	14	28	Sunday
MODERN FAMILY	ABC	7	29	Wednesday
HOUSE HUNTERS	HGTV	42	30	mon-fri
OUTSOURCED	NBC	27	31	Thursday
HELL'S KITCHEN	FOX	37	32	Wednesday
RAISING HOPE	FOX	32	33	Tuesday
CHOPPED	FN	47	34	Tuesday
BROTHERS AND SISTERS	ABC	21	35	Sunday
UNDERCOVER BOSS	CBS	15	36	Sunday
SURVIVOR	CBS	12	37	Wednesday
CASTLE	ABC	9	38	Monday
ACE OF CAKES	FN	53	39	Thursday
THE BIG BANG THEORY	CBS	5	40	Thursday
DINERS, DRIVE-INS, AND DIVES	FN	41	41	Monday
HOW I MET YOUR MOTHER	CBS	19	42	Monday
LAW AND ORDER: SVU	NBC	24	43	Wednesday
NCIS: LOS ANGELES	CBS	8	44	Tuesday
C.S.I. NY	CBS	13	45	Friday
PARENTHOOD	NBC	28	46	Tuesday
CHASE	NBC	33	47	Monday
HAWAII FIVE-O	CBS	11	48	Monday
INCOME PROPERTY	HGTV	50	49	Wednesday
THE MENTALIST	CBS	2	50	Thursday
NO ORDINARY FAMILY	ABC	23	51	Tuesday
THE MIDDLE	ABC	18	52	Wednesday
THE GOOD WIFE	CBS	6	53	Tuesday
SELLING NEW YORK	HGTV	44	54	Thursday

Advertising and marketing nirvana live at the intersection of viewership and the IVR. Large variances between the two metrics spell trouble – on one end or the other. But variances also suggest strategies and tactics. Shows with high viewership and low IVRs (or vice versa) should engage their customers via the social channel – and traditional media – as appropriate. The implications for programming and advertising are broad. There's also an opportunity for serious derivative analysis, where advertisers can not only learn about what viewers are saying about a television program but also the other things they may be talking about. The IVR metric is a powerful way to price advertising time. It's also a path to cross-media communication and engagement.

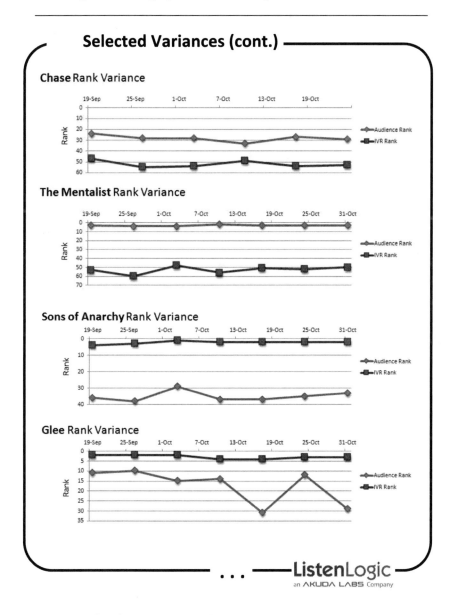

The IVR metric is also extensible to other events and activities, like concerts, exhibits and audio experiences.

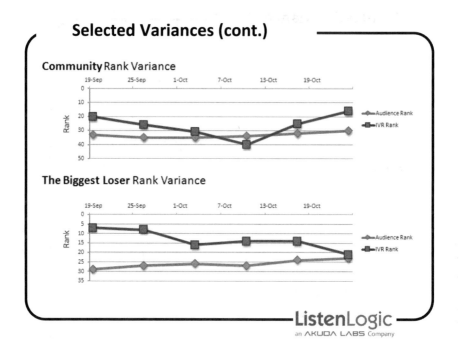

Chapter 9 - Wisk

Wisk is a well-known brand.

There's a surprising amount of conversation about Wisk and other cleaning products. This case looks at traditional surveys versus social business intelligence. It's an especially important case not just because it demonstrates wider and deeper insights than those gained from traditional surveys, but it also demonstrates the synergy between the two methodologies. In other words, while we believe that the power of social business intelligence exceeds that of traditional survey research, we also believe that there's a role for each methodology to play.

A survey conducted on behalf of the Wisk brand was recently published. The findings were the result of a traditional market research survey which asked participants to respond to questions relating to their laundry habits. The focus was "dirty secrets." Levering social business intelligence, ListenLogic conducted its own study of laundry habits, beginning with the universe of laundry conversations and ultimately, isolating and analyzing the "confessions." Which is better? How are surveys and "listening" different?

The Wisk traditional online survey occurred from April 12-19, 2011; the results were published on May 3, 2012:

- Survey was commissioned by Sun Products Corporation for the Wisk Deep Clean and was conducted by Directions Research

- Participants included a national probability sample of 1,000 adults comprising 500 women and 500 men, ages 18-64, living in the Continental United States

- Participants were asked questions regarding their laundry habits

The online survey findings – from 1,000 participants – included:

- Four out of five (approximately 800) admitted to at least one of the following:

- Going more than a month without changing bed sheets

- < 500 wash their sheets on a weekly basis

- Take dirty items out of the laundry basket to wear (more females confess to this activity than men)

- Approximately 1 in 3 women (~ 165) admitted to wearing the same bra several days in a row

- Approximately 1 in 3 men (~ 165) admitted to having worn the same socks or underwear for several days

- "Most people claim(ed) they 'just know' when an item needs to be washed"

But what did the social business intelligence exercise tell us?

The "laundry universe" consisted of consumer conversations referencing laundry and washable items (clothes, towels, sheets, diapers, etc.). Not in the case are consumers referencing laundry in regards to industry and/or professional services i.e., hotels, dry cleaners and coin-operators. Also not included are brand reviews, sales and discounts, references to "airing dirty laundry," gossip or personal things not meant to be shared with others.

Note the number of conversations we found – and the insights we uncovered – in the social business intelligence analysis:

Key Metrics: Laundry

> 1.5 Million Conversations

- Task-related discussions (planning, doing, folding, detergent preferences, etc.) represented 58% of the total volume

- Confessions, 24% of the volume, included personal secrets (*admissions of guilt*) as well as sharing judgments and pet-peeves relating to the habits of others (*accusers*)

- In 12% of the volume, consumers asked questions or offered information

ListenLogic
an AKUDA LABS Company

How about the major themes?

The next figure profiles the frequency of what participants shared about their laundry habits, what they expressed about "smell," what they saw and what they've learned from others in the social conversation about laundry.

Social conversation insights: Laundry

68% (~1M)	39% (~595K)	29% (~440K)	13% (<190K)
Say Share personal laundry habits (good or bad) – i.e. when they do laundry, why and how and with what results	**Smell** Describe smell (good or bad) in relation to laundry and reactions to smells, good & bad	**See** Reference laundry in terms of visual appearance (good or bad for both clean and dirty items.)	**Hear** Share what they've learned from others (good or bad) i.e. health, facts & stats, bad habits, etc.

11% of laundry conversations reference health implications (> 150K)

ListenLogic
an AKUDA LABS Company

What else?

Additional Insights: Laundry

"Gross" – 7% of the Total Laundry Conversations Reference the Relationship Between Dirty Laundry & Health (~ 110K of 1,510,000)

- When referencing a correlation between laundry and health, consumers most commonly discussed one of the following:

- Conditions the consumer (or household member) was currently experiencing (i.e., acne, allergies, and skin irritation) which they associated with bad laundry habits (27,000)

- What the consumer could "catch" from someone that had bad laundry habits (lice, bedbugs, STD): consumers correlated bad laundry habits with poor hygiene practices (~ 56,000)

- Concerns regarding pets in beds were referenced in approximately 11,000 conversations

The Wisk personas appear below. Six groups dominated the laundry discussion

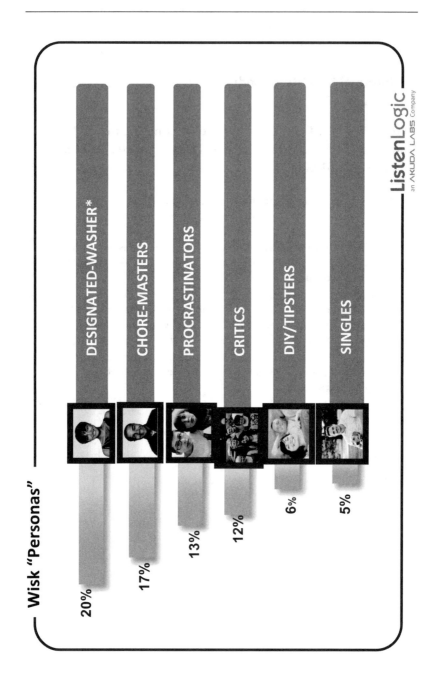

What else did we learn?

"Persona" Insights: Wisk

- "Confessions" (Guilty Party admitted a "Dirty Secret" & Accuser described

- pet-peeves or judgments) were found in 24% of the total laundry conversations (369,255 of 1,510,776)

- Bad laundry habits impacted the offenders relationships and image

- Pet-peeves typically referenced family members and highlighted how someone else's bad habits are impacting them (the person with a pet-peeve)

- When sharing judgments, the consequences typically impacted the person with bad habits – directly i.e., didn't get the job offer or indirectly i.e., influenced reputation

- Dirty Secrets (habits) were not so secret: 65% of conversations referenced a specific individual with whom the accuser had direct or indirect contact

- 38% of the judgments referenced a personal acquaintance and shared the person's name or how they are acquainted (~ 53,000 of 139,453)

- Consumer conversations revealed the consequences of having bad laundry habits

- Impacted established relationships – roommates, marriage and other romantic relationships (> 70,000)

- Negatively impacted first impressions – strangers, first dates, work colleagues and interviews; a reflection of parenting skills (> 50,000)

. . .

"Persona" Insights: Wisk (cont.)

Health

- Consumers discussed conditions (i.e., acne, allergies and skin irritation) that they associated with bad laundry habits (27,000)

- Health-related conversations referenced what the consumer could "catch" from someone that had bad laundry habits: consumers correlated bad laundry habits with poor hygiene practices (~ 56,000)

- Concerns regarding pets in beds are referenced in approximately 11,000 conversations

- Of the most common confessions, the most common includes knowingly wearing something that was not clean by the consumer's standards

ListenLogic
an AKUDA LABS Company

So how did the two approaches compare?

What are the essential differences?

Traditional Survey versus Social Intelligence

Airing Dirty Laundry

- Survey Said: 4 out of 5 admitted to being guilty of at least one Dirty Laundry Secret

- Social Intelligence Said: Confessions were found in 24% of the total laundry conversation; most commonly confessed, *knowingly wearing something that is not clean* (doesn't meet the consumer's personal standards)

Insight:
➢ Social Intelligence verified that *dirty secrets* and *bad habits* are indeed commonplace; it also confirmed that people understand that there is a difference between good and bad habits

. . .
ListenLogic
an AKUDA LABS Company

122

Traditional Survey versus Social Intelligence (cont.)

Tangible Testing Identifies Dirty Laundry

- Survey Said: "Most people claim(ed) they 'just know' when an item needs to be washed"

- Social Intelligence Said: Whether speaking as the guilty party or the accuser, consumers described "how" they know if an item is dirty (needs to be washed) by way of "testing"

Insight:

➢ When sharing Dirty Secrets, 36% of conversations referenced "testing" the item to determine whether it was okay to use without washing

➢ In 90% of these posts, the consumer indicated they tested for tangible evidence – visual inspection (for stains or wrinkles) and smell-testing; an additional 4% referenced "feel"

Dirty Laundry = Gross

- Survey Said: "What they (consumers who 'just know' when laundry is dirty) may not know was that the average wash load contains 20 times more body oils and sweat than the visible stain

- Social Intelligence Said: As related to health, less than 1% of the confessions referenced "trapped oils" (or contaminants); when referencing dirty laundry with disgust, consumers referenced concerns relating to infections or contagious conditions i.e. lice, STDs and bed bugs; of the judgment conversations, 5% of posts correlated bad laundry habits with poor hygiene

Insight:

➢ The findings included specific information regarding "what" is found in unwashed laundry – an assumption that consumers will find this to be "gross"; consumers however, did not demonstrate an interest in "what" was in the laundry – "gross" referenced the end result

. . .

Traditional Survey versus Social Intelligence (cont.)

Defining "Bad Habit"

- Survey Said: There was an assumption made that (female) consumers understood that bras should be washed after each use and that *multiple wears between washing reflected a "poor habit"*

- Social Intelligence: Women described wearing the same bra multiple times before washing; *however, social revealed that women do not consider this a bad habit*

Insight:

➢ Consumers did not necessarily identify multiple wears between washing as being a bad habit; consumers described awareness of the importance of washing but frequency was the issue: "clean" was a universal reference

Self-Awareness and Consequences

- Survey Said: Four out of five consumers confessed to at least one Dirty Secret and most consumers "just knew" if something needed to be cleaned

- Social Intelligence Said: Within the confessions, less than 1% of guilty consumers indicated that the *Secret* was exposed (awareness that one or more people noticed the guilty parties' habit); consumers were under the false impression that their secret was safe; Accusers shared harsh critiques in response to noticing *stains* or *smells* (> 80% of the judgments); Accusers described the impact on relationships, employment, first-impressions, image and reputation

Insight:

➢ Consumers were not as good as they thought when it came to identifying what needs to be washed; more importantly, discovery resulted in significant negative consequences

. . .

Traditional Survey versus Social Intelligence (cont.)

Bad Habits Extend Beyond Frequency of Wash

- Survey Said: *"If your family is guilty* (of a listed bad habit related to using dirty items) ... *you're not alone"* – the survey implied that *bad habit* means using items more than once between washes (or going over one week without washing sheets)

- Social Intelligence Said: The confession conversation defined bad habits in more a general sense – using or wearing stained or "smelly" items

Insight:

➤ Regularly washing clothes but failing to identify that the detergent was ineffective (does not "deep clean" or eliminate *Ring Around the Collar*™) was judged as a bad habit, *but this practice was not something participants were asked about* ... and this is the Wisk® Deep Clean™ value proposition!

ListenLogic
an AKUDA LABS Company

Part III

Social Business Intelligence Today & Tomorrow

Chapter 10 - Social Business Intelligence (SBI) Due Diligence

Why is social so compelling?

There are five characteristics that make SBI possible – and productive:

The first is **reach**: As of this writing (2012), Facebook has more than 900,000,000 users and Twitter has over 275,000,000. Over 500,000,000 use YouTube monthly. Facebook is still growing, and Twitter is growing even faster. In addition to these platforms are thousands of others that have specific missions (like travel, sports, politics, health, etc.). These platforms are also growing dramatically: every likes to talk; everyone has an opinion.

According to Neal O'Farrell (way back in 2011), "In The Headlines: Exactly How Big Is Facebook?," September 6, 2011, at: http://www.idguardian.com/headlines-facebook/and http://askaaronlee.com/twitter-users/:

> *"More than 250 million of Facebook users access Facebook through their mobile devices. 50% of active Facebook users log in on any given day. The average Facebook user has 130 friends, is connected to 80 community pages, groups and events, and creates 90 pieces of content each month. People around the world spend over 700 billion combined minutes on Facebook pages every month. And exactly what are all these people doing on Facebook? Viewing more than 900 million pages, groups, events, and community pages. Or browsing through more than 30 billion Web links, news stories, blog posts, notes, photo albums and other content. And they're probably using the more than 20 million applications installed every day on Facebook, created by an army of entrepreneurs in more than 190 countries."*

The second characteristic is **credibility**: we know that just about everyone believes what their friends tell them versus what paid talking heads tell anyone. While social media is full of strange and inaccurate tweets, blogs and posts, it's also full of honest insight and thoughts.

After decades of "false advertising" and very little regulation around what advertiser's say or do, the perfect storm has created a communications and collaboration channel that's also unregulated – *but perceived as much more credible.*

The third is **ubiquity and pervasiveness**: the stage is set for continuous listening – and the analysis of what we hear. We've never had such access to customers, suppliers, employees, partners and competitors. "Release-and-listen" is the new product/service development strategy. "Listen-or-die" is the new customer service mantra.

The fourth characteristic is **volume**: where no one would want to develop a corporate strategy based on a few posts on a few social media sites, when there are thousands of posts a week on major (and minor) brands, products and services, it's easy to infer sentiment (and more) and trajectory and then craft reactive and proactive responses. As volume grows – which it inevitably will – more and more use will be made of social media data, since volume statistically validates the inferences and conclusions companies require regarding their products and services.

The fifth is **demographics**: while social media has been embraced by all age groups, generations X and Y are major participants and will continue to be so throughout their lives. (Generation Z will not differentiate social media from media of any kind and will seamlessly integrate social media-based communication and collaboration into their personal and professional lives.) *Put another way, the future is about social media, just as the past was about email and transactional corporate Web sites.*

Social media should work with structured data about customers, sales, manufacturing and service by providing insights, explanations and prescriptions: social media optimizes business intelligence (BI) investments. Social media is about integrating unstructured with structured data about products, customers, service, brand management, innovation and all things that touch every aspect of your physical and digital supply chain.

Social business intelligence is not just about listening to Twitter. It's not about listening to the nice things being said about your company. It's not locating social media listening in a business silo. There is governance around social media and SBI. There are also technology and acquisition issues, like whether a company should build an in-house SBI capability or whether it should find a partner that listens and analyzes on behalf of the company. In fact, there are many issues, opportunities and risks associated with SBI. Let's look at ten of the most critical to optimizing SBI.

1. All Social Data Is Not Created Equal

The sheer volume of social media data scares even the most capable database manager. So many companies and their social media listening partners *only sample social media data streams* with (sometimes small) subsets of posts, tweets and blogs used to (only) profile sentiment, customer service and brands.

Not everyone is aware that social media data is frequently purchased by social media listening companies. The listening companies do this because collecting/ filtering/ structuring social media data is not their core competency (even though they are social media listening companies!). They also do this because even if they could collect all of the data they need to fulfill client requirements, the cost of doing so is often too high for them to remain profitable – so they sample rather than collect all social media data.

They also search social media sites awkwardly, usually with only client-provided keywords that are difficult if not impossible to separate from "noise." The proverbial signal-to-noise problem is huge – and growing – with social media data. The vast majority of posts, tweets and blogs are of little or no use to specific company needs. It's therefore important to find the right signals. But doing so requires a social media collection/ filtering/ structuring capability that very few social media listening companies actually have – in spite of what they might tell their clients.

Managers and executives should also understand that most social media listening companies get only partial feeds from sites like Twitter and Facebook and don't go deep into the Web to collect the hard-to-find communities and industry-related websites relevant to their clients' businesses. This is because most of the most relevant websites are extremely difficult to penetrate for social data collection and because they don't have simple RSS filters (really simple syndication) and API (application programming interface) feeds. So the social media listening companies just don't hear them. This is a major data collection problem.

Another "all-data's-not-created-equal" issue is data filtering. Most keyword-based social media tools do not take natural language processing, semantic analysis, concept clustering and context into consideration. Charts and graphs are important, but only when they represent data that's meaningful. Social media data analysis should yield clear influence hierarchies, that is, insights into who the most influential authors/publishers are – and are not. It should also be possible to identify gender, location, political affiliation and other profile characteristics from tweets, blogs and posts. A robust social media collection/filtering/structuring engine will embellish the data with verifiable extensions that add richness to the analyses that everyone wants to perform.

Finally, it should be possible to not only collect all of the data your clients need, categorize it, enhance it *and* structure it, but also prepare it for additional use in enterprise CRM, BI and data base management (DBM) platforms. This last capability is essential to extending the power of social media data and integrating it into the processes and software applications that so many companies have deployed. (This is discussed in more detail below.)

So what should a social media listening company be able to do with data? Here's a representative list of basic capabilities:

- Data Processing: the set of machines, processor cores, memory, storage capacity and network bisection bandwidth composing the platform that executes all processes.

- Data Harvesting: refers to the mechanisms used to gather data from social networks, forums, blogs, and the Web in general. The mechanisms include paid data aggregation services, source-defined APIs (application programming interfaces), and site-specific scrapers, among other collection techniques.

- Data Storage: refers to a scalable storage system, normally in the form of a database management system (DBMS) and hard (or solid-state) disks attached to the physical machines via different types of links, with different levels of bandwidth and latency.

- Data Filtering: lexical and semantic adaptive filters dedicated to sifting through a global Internet fire-hose, letting through only those items that are relevant to a specific topic. Topics can be extremely narrow or extremely broad.

- Data Indexing: scalable global data search indexes used for old data analysis. These indexes should be global or topic-specific.

- Data Analysis: enables the analysis of all collected filtered data to answer the questions associate with a topic.

- Data Delivery: delivers data and the results of the data analysis.

- Interactive Research: allows humans monitoring a topic to do more in-depth data analysis through the execution of queries or feedback into the learning engines of the data analysis system.

- When all is said and done, a social media listening company should be able to:

- Collect 100's of millions of data snippets daily

- Classify, index and store 100's of millions of items/day in real time, with average latency times of 40 milliseconds

- Use lexical, semantic and statistical filters

- Use machine learning techniques to continuously improve data filters

- Extract author and publisher information; harvest demographics and augment demographics through the use of statistical models and machine learning techniques

- Use supercomputing, multi-level systolic pipelines and map-reduce (beyond the capabilities of Hadoop), cloud resource scheduling, process migration, 1000's of CPU's, terabytes of memory and petabytes of storage

These capabilities permit the collection, filtering, analysis and structuring of deep, relevant social media data.

Without these capabilities, procuring companies will travel an expensive path to modest results.

2. Social Data Must Integrate

Integration and interoperability are always on the short list of capabilities that technologists and savvy managers require. Managers define integration around processes, while technologists define it around their technology hardware platforms, software applications and databases. In order for integration to be effective, it must satisfy both definitions.

Processes around customer service, for example, are traditionally defined around client services, conflict resolution and larger supply chain efficiencies, which means that social process integration needs to occur within existing functions, such as CRM, brand management, customer service, innovation and crisis management. These are only some of the functions impacted by social media. In CRM, for example, social customer relationship management (SCRM) assumes the collection, analysis and inspection of social media data. It assumes that social media data is used to add depth to the analysis of customer relationships, to add explanatory power around why customers buy more – or less – and yield to up-selling and cross-selling opportunities.

In order for social media data to be impactful, the analytical processes around key functions must be modified to include social data. This requires process changes *and* process governance. Companies that fail to modify their functional processes and the governance that supports them will fail to integrate social media into their operating models. On the technology side, things are more complicated. Note that process always precedes technology so technology integration should stand on the shoulders of process integration. That said, for social media data to be impactful it must integrate into the primary analytical and transactional platforms that medium and large enterprises have deployed, platforms such as CRM, BI, statistical analysis, ERP and DBM, and others that power so many companies. This means that social media data should feed these platforms and integrate into the analytical processes the platforms support.

This is no easy feat. Enterprise platforms are notoriously fickle when it comes to integration: proprietary software applications seldom cooperate with one another. Social media listening companies need to understand the structures and processes of numerous software applications – after they structure all of the unstructured social data they collect and filter. In the trenches this means that structured social media data must integrate with at least the major platforms such as those from IBM, Oracle, SAP, SAS and Microsoft. Within these vendors' worlds are various CRM, BI, statistical analysis, ERP and DBM platforms each with their own unique technology and process integration requirements. Social media teams must be able to feed these platforms as though social media data was made to seamlessly integrate into their technology and functional operating models.

A capable social media listening team should therefore be able to perform the following integration tasks:

- Define social process definitions across major corporate functional areas

- Structure filtered social media data

- Integrate structured/filtered social media data into enterprise platforms such as CRM, BI, statistical and DBM software applications represented by the major technology vendors

3. Social Media Can Be Modeled

Social media data is sometimes perceived as random, disjointed and inconsistent chatter about brands, products and services. One of the myths about social media is that it's only for kids who like to announce their presence at their favorite bars, for chronic complainers and for grandparents connecting with their kids and grandkids. In fact, social media data can reveal much more about what customers, employees and suppliers think, believe and feel: social media data – when expertly modeled – can yield explanatory and predictive insight that otherwise would simply fall between the analytical cracks of keyword-based social media listening.

What can be modeled?

Can social media, for example, reveal insight into the state of a company's "wellness"? Can a diagnostic set of social media indicators of corporate wellness (growth and decline) be identified and validated? Can traditional empirical corporate performance metrics be integrated with social media indicators to build comprehensive predictive models of corporate wellness? Can specific wellness outcomes be correlated with social media? Can Twitter feeds predict behavior, such as box-office receipts, new product success and the next fad?

Examples of social media posts that would indicate corporate health – or illness – include (positive or negative) references to the senior management team, the failure (or success) of new products, audit problems, revenue projections, quality problems, office closings, layoffs, hiring, new store openings, and bill collection notices, among countless others. The modeling challenge is to identify the combinations of indicators that reveal predictive patterns.

Tweets have already been used to measure movie sentiment and box-office revenue with amazing accuracy. Note the work of Asur and Bernardo who predicted the movie "Dear John" would earn $30.71 million at the box office on its opening weekend. It actually generated $30.46 million. For the movie "The Crazies," they predicted a $16.8 million opening: it generated $16.07 million. According to the authors of the National Science Foundation (NSF)-supported study,

> *"We use the chatter from Twitter.com to forecast box-office revenues for movies. We show that a simple model built from the rate at which tweets are created about particular topics can outperform market-based predictors. We further demonstrate how sentiments extracted from Twitter can be further utilized to improve the forecasting power of social media."* (See Sitaram Asur and Bernardo A. Huberman, *Predicting the Future With Social Media*, Web Intelligence and Intelligent Agent Technology (WIIAT), 2010 IEEE/WIC /ACM International Conference Social Computing Lab., HP Labs., Palo Alto, CA, USA, August 31, 2010-September 3, 2010 for more information on social media modeling. Also see www.hpl.hp.com/research/scl/papers/socialmedia/socialmedia.pdf.)

Social media can predict a wide range of events and behaviors. The military is looking at social media for I&W, the early prediction of unpleasant global events. Companies are using social media to predict if a new sneaker will soar – or crash – and analysts are tapping into social media blogs, tweets and posts to determine the timing and nature of whole social movements. As suggested in Chapter 1, who can deny the impact that social media has had on global political events like what we've recently seen in Iran, Egypt and Libya? The power that Facebook and Twitter demonstrated in those countries is amazing. What about corporate interests in these countries? The global "Occupy" movement is another example of just how powerful – and predictive – social media is.

What about electoral politics? What constituents say about their representatives is of enormous value – and risk – to politicians. Social media has become a communications channel that politicians cannot control, but can influence. "Social models" are under development that are initially proving to be every bit as predictive as proverbial survey and focus group data. Note the results of early research of Andranik Tumasjan, Timm O. Sprenger, Philopp G. Sandner and Isabel M. Welpe, "Predicting Elections with Twitter," International Conference on WebLogs & Social Media, Washington, DC, USA, May 25, 2010 for additional information on election modeling; also see "Can Social Media Predict the Election Results?,"http://www.prweb.com/releases/2010/10/prweb4641374.h tm, New York, NY (PRWEB) October 13, 2010. Also see: http://www.electionarena.com:

"In the Senate Primary Races, winners of 8 of the 10 contested Senate primary races were predicted by the number of Facebook supporters the candidates had a week before the elections. Similarly, in the Congressional Primary Races, winners of 42 of the 57 contested Congressional primary races were predicted by the number of Facebook supporters. Are these findings indicative? Campaigning on the internet and social media has been widely discussed as a potential catalyst for grassroots action and social change. As a prediction tool, future studies will tell whether online social networks can act as a proxy for predicting election results. As The Economist *noted, the power of traditional polls in predicting election results has been declining since fewer Americans have landline phones, making the population samples pollsters use more and more prone to statistical biases."*

The end-game is the identification, combination and validation of social indicators predictive of specific events, behaviors and conditions. Ideally, these "soft" indicators are combined with more traditional empirical indicators to develop robust predictive models that can explain and forecast a variety of events, behaviors and conditions.

Social media teams should have the ability to do the following:

- Identify diagnostic behavioral indicators

- Develop explanatory and predictive models across industries

- Validate adaptive explanatory and predictive models

Listening teams without these capabilities can only provide limited interpretations of what they hear.

4. Derivative Analytics

The world is amass in predictive analytics (PA) vendors, white papers and case studies. PA has always been about predicting what, where and when – regardless of the domain. BI is actually now a subset of PA – not the other way around as it conceptually should be. But there's another dimension to BI/PI that social media data enables: derivative analytics (DA). While there's always a reluctance to crown yet another analytical area – especially when we're still not too sure where BI ends and PA begins – social media provides a first, second, third and Nth-order context to feelings, beliefs and behavior. Understanding the nature and trajectory of the social crowd is huge, which enables additional primary, secondary and Nth-order analyses.

Here's an example of DA. If you listen to what readers of *Cosmopolitan Magazine* are saying about the magazine you will quickly learn what they like and don't like, what articles they find most useful and the clothes they absolutely must buy. The cover of "Cosmo" is always the subject of blogs, tweets and posts – especially if it has a celebrity sporting a special outfit (which it usually does). But if you listen closely, you can infer much more than what's literally being said. It's possible to profile the conversationalists by gender (almost all are female), age, physical location, time of day, race, religious orientation, influence and other variables that together describe the total conversational context, which is what enables DA. In the case of Cosmo readers, it's possible to know exactly what they're doing when they read the magazine. They might be drinking tea, polishing their nails, shaving their legs, talking to their mothers, Face-timing their friends, texting, or eating pizza. What if a preponderance of readers were doing many of the same things and what if *Cosmo* only advertised in a few of the active areas? Social evidence that, for example, 22% of all *Cosmo* readers read in bed while drinking tea provides an immediate opportunity for tea vendors of all kinds to showcase their wares to an audience predisposed to what they're selling. Showcasing could be directly in the magazine, on the *Cosmo* web site, and through *Cosmo* tweets, blogs and posts to their fans about all of the tea merchandise they might purchase. For this empirical targeted audience – validated by DA – *Cosmo* could charge its advertisers more than it now does.

Similarly, the entertainment industry's DA might focus on what people are saying about specific movies, television programs, commercials, concerts and radio spots. Tweets, posts and blog entries can add depth and color to commentary on various entertainment venues, but they can also provide additional insights into viewer/listener involvement and from those inferences, which content is the most valuable to artists and advertisers, among other target groups. Social media can help correlate viewer/listener involvement with all sorts of activity through the gathering and analysis of social media intelligence. As suggested in Chapter 8, this kind of analysis can revolutionize the way we think about entertainment ratings, which will evolve from "what did you watch at 10PM" to "how involved were you in what you watched at 10PM" based on your participation in social media before, during and after your viewing of/listening to specific content.

What someone says, what someone means and what someone does in the context of a literal post, tweet or blog is the essence of DA. Maps that describe and follow conversations reveal opportunities and risks for companies, brand managers and marketers looking to mine social media data as widely and deeply as possible. DA is discover-able, not predictably model-able. But patterns can be observed and defined as they emerge. They also repeat themselves. While it's impossible to predict that movie goers will – after watching the opening scene of a film about restaurants – become hungry for Crème Brulee, it is possible to observe it – and respond for a variety of business purposes.

The key is context. The wider and deeper the social context in which the data is interpreted the more inferences can be made. Since social conversations are by nature multi-dimensional – with multiple simultaneous conversations occurring continuously – there are numerous ways to parse conversational trajectories, content and purposes. We've learned that a Web site where new babies are discussed is also the site where weight loss and part-time work is discussed. The trick is to understand that what passes as focused discussion on one site is actually opportunistically unfocused since there are no rules about what can or cannot be posted, tweeted or blogged. The ability to travel down these endless conversational paths and extract meaning and purpose is a core competency of the best social media listening companies. Unfortunately, many listening companies do not have the ability to conduct DA.

Social media vendors should have the following DA abilities:

- Track, parse and profile multiple conversations simultaneously

- Contextualize conversations well beyond initial or trigger content and discussions

- Infer from multiple levels of analysis

These capabilities are critical to extending the diagnostic usefulness of SBI.

5. Social Media is Internal, External, Active & Passive

Much of the focus of social media is external – on what customers are saying and what competitors are doing. But lots of social media occurs within companies among their employees, suppliers and partners. It's important to remember that social media includes all stakeholders, all the time.

We also tend to think more about social media listening than social media engagement. In fact, one of the primary reasons to listen is to reactively and pro-actively engage stakeholders.

The following figure presents the matrix that, in turns, suggests where social media investments should be made. A comprehensive social media strategy (discussed below) acknowledges the importance of all four cells in the matrix.

All cells in the matrix are created equal – in spite of most of the emphasis placed on external versus internal and listening versus engagement. Employee demographics require companies to not only listen to their employees but to enable their social preferences by providing social technology and processes that encourage social media-based communication and collaboration. Suppliers and partners also require social media capabilities – and all of the internal social activity should be ananlyzed across all sorts of behavior and performance metrics.

The external listening imperative is clear and companies have embraced the need to listen to their customers and competitors. The engagement challenge is more complicated, especially since it depends on the quality of listening data collected, filtered, classified and analyzed.

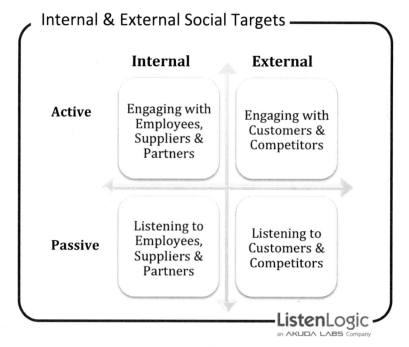

Engagement requires an approach that is – like customer service – focused on relationship-building. When a customer applauds or complains about a product or service, what should the response be? How should a response be structured? What "if-then" rules should apply? For example, if a customer complains three times about an experience with a company – and that customer is wealthy and socially influential – how, when and in what form should that customer be engaged? Put another way, engagement is much more complicated than posting coupons on Groupon. In fact, engagement runs the gamut of proactive and reactive approaches to SBI. Among other things, social media can help design, test and deploy products and product enhancements.

Why would a company believe it absolutely knows what its customers want? Why not ask them – via social media – along an engagement continuum? Why not try before they build – via social media? Innovation is also a proactive opportunity. Why not ask anyone and everyone about what's new? Open innovation is, in fact, based on social media crowdsourcing.

Listening is unfulfilled social media; engagement converts listening into strategies and tactics. Both listening and engagement are internal and external pastimes. Social media teams should have the following internal/external/active/passive abilities:

- Segment social media activities and targets with appropriate business processes and technologies that optimize listening and engagement opportunities

- Develop suites of internal/external/active/passive strategies and tactics designed to find the right listening and engagement combinations

- Pilot alternative listening/engagement opportunities, especially in areas that exploit the collaboration/connectivity strengths of social media, like crowdsourcing

These capabilities are essential to developing holistic listening-to-analysis-to-engagement approaches to SBI.

6. Real-Time Versus Old-Time

Some events and processes require real-time listening and response. The whole world of threat tracking and crisis management is one of the most significant real-time areas. As already mentioned, how many companies drive themselves into a ditch? Just about all of them at one time or another. How deep is the ditch? What's the best way to get out of it? Is it getting bigger? These are just a few of the questions that require real-time social media.

Definitions are important when discussing real-time, near-real-time and slow(er)-time. Real-time is *real-time*: immediate, with extremely low latency. Near-real-time often refers to response times that are delayed by some measurable increment that can range from minutes to hours or even days. Responses that are weeks old are not near-real-time. Slower-time reporting can range from days to months.

Real-time listening is essential for a range of activities, behaviors and events that create corporate risk – or unique opportunities. Threat analysis is an obvious example of the need for real-time listening. Certain financial events also require real-time listening and engagement. Real-time is useful when action, reaction and engagement are immediately required to mitigate some event or condition, or to capitalize on some special opportunity.

While some real-time requirements are easy to understand, others are not. Financial events often require real-time reporting as do the announcements and initiatives of key competitors.

Management must decide about the need for real-time SBI by taking the following steps:

- Identify the events, behaviors and conditions that qualify as real-time targets

- Build or buy a real-time listening/engagement capability

- Develop "what-if"/"if-then" scenarios for real-time listening/engagement

7. Man Versus Machine

This is a perennial issue especially as expectations about automation grow. The allocation of tasks across analysts and algorithms is a moving target, since automation technologies continue to improve. The old arguments about what machines can and cannot do rage on. Some believe that there are tasks that only humans can perform; others believe that it's only a matter of time before even the most complex tasks – like flying and landing aircraft – are completely automated.

Social media is complicated and requires two-dimensional domain depth. The first refers to the language and "conversation" of social media, while the second refers to the domains to which social media applies. There are countless words, phrases and abbreviations, among other language artifacts, that enable social media conversations. While many of these artifacts can be interpreted by smart machines, others are not so easily deciphered.

The vertical domains in which social media occurs are also complicated. There are whole lexicons (different from the social media language and communications artifacts) for vertical business domains that require an understanding of the domains that's difficult to comprehensively code in a software application – regardless of how "intelligent" it might be. The retail, pharmaceutical, manufacturing, financial services, insurance, entertainment and chemical industries, among others, have unique processes, histories, best practices, trajectories, cost models and even customer service protocols – among other differences – that require an understanding that machines can interpret at a deductive level but never at an inductive one. We are still some years away from comprehensive vertical knowledge representation so it's necessary to augment whatever artificial intelligence that exists with targeted organic intelligence.

All of this means that there's a necessary social media partnership between man and machine. It's impossible – for now, at least – to expect machines to have deductive and inductive knowledge about every vertical industry, or for machines to comprehend and interpret every language artifact for all social conversationalists – especially since they change all the time. Human analysts are a necessary part of the SBI process. Note that this is no different from what governments have acknowledged for years as they listen to what their global competitors are doing. Their "I&W" operations have relied on both men and machines to forecast global events for decades. While the machines get smarter and smarter, there's no substitute for the insight and analysis that subject matter experts (SMEs) can provide.

Perhaps the riskiest social media listening practice is keyword-based listening, where keywords are expected to yield the most insightful analysis without deep contextual domain or social language understanding. Machines may be good at finding keywords from sampled social media data streams, but they're far from perfect at interpreting what the keywords mean or using keyword-based listening to engage customers or predict events. Better collection/filtering/structuring can help a lot, but the more complicated the data the more we need subject matter experts to participate in the whole SBI process.

Social media vendors – or an in-house social media listening/engaging team – should have the ability to do the following:

- Allocate SBI tasks along a man-machine continuum that realistically assigns the right tasks to the right agent

- Recognize – and invest in – a balanced man-machine SBI platform

- Continuously assess the state of SBI automation, especially as it pertains to vertical industry knowledge representation

8. Acquiring Social Business Intelligence

The age-old technology acquisition question applies to social media listening and analysis: build or buy? When Salesforce.com bought the social media listening company Radian6, it announced that social listening would move to the Salesforce.com cloud, where clients could rent a tool that would perform keyword searches whenever and wherever they wanted. Other social media tool companies have the same approach. But some others see social media as more complex, requiring some supporting analysis to fully understand what the social conversations mean especially across very different industries.

There are several social media acquisition options. The first option is classic: build an internal social media listening capability by hiring and training professionals, build/license/acquire social media listening (and analytical) technology, and develop internal processes for leveraging social media across the enterprise.

The second option is consistent with emerging acquisition and deployment best practices, as cloud computing rises in popularity and improves its capabilities. More and more companies are renting listening and engagement technologies and expertise rather than building those capabilities in-house.

The question for companies interested in mining social media is one of commitment and urgency. If a company declares SBI as a future core competency, it might commit to an in-house development effort, but if urgency is part of the equation the same company might rent a tool to get their feet wet as quickly as possible.

There are also hybrid acquisition models that combine aspects of core competency and urgency decision criteria, among others. Some companies might, for example, purchase large amounts of social media data, hire a vendor to build some interfaces to their CRM platforms, then build an internal analytical capability to optimize SBI. Companies might also hire consultants to build models that their in-house statistical packages might run, or integrate data into their BI platforms.

Many companies today are defaulting to small initial projects that test the value of social media listening and engagement, but the real question is not the build versus buy one, or even the hybrid one. The real question is about expertise and it's optimal location.

Social Media Capabilities & Acquisition Options

Capabilities & Acquisition Options	Data Collection & Filtering	Integration	Modeling	Derivative Analytics	Internal/ External/ Listen/ Engage	Real-Time	Man Versus Machine	Measure-ment	Social Media Strategy
In-House									
Outsourced									
Hybrid									

ListenLogic
an AKUDA LABS Company

The following matrix helps with an acquisition options assessment. Some best practices are emerging that should help companies decide how and what they want to acquire. Best SBI practices also suggest that modeling, derivative analytics (DA), internal/external/listening/engagement campaigns, man-machine task allocation, measurement and social media strategy be developed in-house. The hybrid areas include modeling, DA, and man-versus-machine task allocation – all as suggested in the matrix. These three areas could stay in-house or be outsourced.

Management should understand the range of social media skills and capabilities and how they should best acquire them:

- Define core competencies around technology generally and social media specifically

- Identify the specific social media capabilities necessary to deliver SBI

- Develop and implement a sourcing strategy that optimizes core competency and SBI requirements

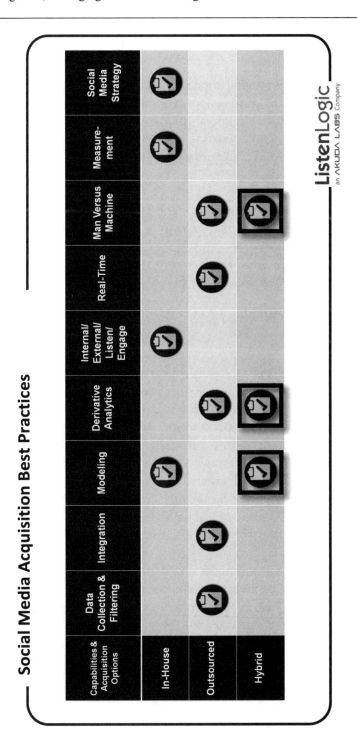

Social Media Acquisition Best Practices

ListenLogic
an AKUDA LABS Company

Capabilities & Acquisition Options	Data Collection & Filtering	Integration	Modeling	Derivative Analytics	Internal/ External/ Listen/ Engage	Real-Time	Man Versus Machine	Measure-ment	Social Media Strategy
In-House	✓	✓	✓		✓			✓	✓
Outsourced				✓			✓	✓		
Hybrid			✓	✓				✓		

9. Measurement

Social media investment impact must be measured. Business cases should be developed and vetted across the management team to assure support. Social media impact metrics should fall into at least two broad categories: total cost of ownership (TCO) and return on investment (ROI), and each of these categories should be further delineated.

TCO is a traditional metric that identifies and tracks all costs connected with an initiative. Perhaps the most notorious TCO metric is the annual cost of Blackberry support for each employee ($4,250 annually as famously reported by the Gartner Group). ROI is the business impact metric that assesses costs versus benefit.

TCO is a driver of ROI, but business performance metrics are the essence of ROI calculations.

Social media is not an especially expensive endeavor. When compared to the largest enterprise technology projects – like ERP, CRM, BI or network and systems management projects – social media is downright cheap. Even the most comprehensive TCO models that include everything that a company might spend on social media will not reveal especially large sums of money – unless a company decides, based on its core competency assessment, that it needs a large sophisticated in-house social media listening and engagement capability. If a company outsources significant parts of its SBI initiative, it's TCO will not be high. The larger question centers around ROI.

ROI is about business impact, so the metrics need to address before-and-after effects of investments in social media "presence," like with Facebook and Twitter (and numerous other platforms), and social media engagement, especially with existing and prospective customers. Traditional metrics around sales, customer service, physical and digital visits, etc. will define the impact of social media initiatives.

As with all useful ROI calculations, companies should begin with metrics aligned to their social media investment objectives. In the short run, these objectives speak to simple activities, like the number of "Likes" on a Facebook page, but longer-term the metrics should speak to objectives that assume that social media is here to stay and will become a continuous communications and collaboration channel.

- Management should focus on TCO and ROI, as follows:

- Develop a comprehensive social media TCO model

- Develop an aligned (to business objectives and requirements) social media ROI model

Distinguish between short-term and longer-term TCO and ROI metrics and adapt calculations to initial social media initiatives and longer-term continuous listening/engagement requirements as the social media channel inevitably becomes permanent

10. Social Business Intelligence Requires a Strategy

How can a company *not* invest in social media? While we spend billions every year on BI, shouldn't we also spend some money on *social* BI? Companies also spend heavily on innovation, focus groups, competitor intelligence and brand management: social media can add a significant dimension of understanding, analysis and action to all of these activities and more. It's also extremely cost-effective. As suggested above, companies can build their own social media listening/responding teams, or contract with any number of vendors that provide social media listening services at fees ranging from the low thousands to the high tens of thousands a month.

Companies should identify opportunities to leverage social media data, information and knowledge by focusing on internal and external processes, functions and objectives. Internal opportunities leverage the same tools companies can use for external SBI. The key is to identify the social media tools likely to have the most impact on a set of internal and external activities that will generate measurable business value.

External activities include listening-for-purpose and more specific activities include market research, brand and marketing intelligence, competitive intelligence, product innovation and life cycle management, customer service, customer relationship management, innovation, reputation management and threat tracking, among other areas. Internal activities include listening to and engaging with employees, suppliers and partners.

Companies should develop strategies that will define their objectives and the means to achieve them:

- Identify the business objectives and requirements wide and deep enough to support the development of a viable social media investment strategy

- Identify the questions whose answers constitute a strategy

- Adapt the strategy to investment results

The Social Business Intelligence Due Diligence Checklist

Developing a *bona fide* SBI capability is difficult because the breadth and depth of skills and competencies are expensive to build in-house – and hard to find in a single vendor. Data capabilities are the most important set of due diligence criteria: if a team only samples social media data streams and finds it difficult to filter, expand, structure and/or integrate social media data into primary and secondary software applications then it's probably a good idea to develop (or find) wider and deeper basic data skills.

At the end of the day, a social media team should be able to the following – which constitutes a due diligence checklist for management:

- Collect 100's of millions of data snippets daily
- Extract author and publisher information; harvest demographics and augment demographics through the use of statistical models and machine learning techniques

- Use machine learning techniques to continuously improve data filters

- Use lexical, semantic and statistical filters

- Classify, index and store 100's of millions of items/day in real time, with average latency times of 40 milliseconds

- Use supercomputing, multi-level systolic pipelines and map-reduce (beyond the capabilities of Hadoop), cloud resource scheduling, process migration, 1000's of CPU's, terabytes of memory and petabytes of storage

- Define social process definitions across major corporate functional areas

- Structure filtered social media data

- Integrate structured/filtered social media data into enterprise platforms such as CRM, BI, statistical and DBM software applications represented by the major technology vendors

- Identify diagnostic behavioral indicators

- Develop explanatory and predictive models across industries

- Validate adaptive explanatory and predictive models

- Track, parse and profile multiple conversations simultaneously

- Contextualize conversations well beyond initial or trigger content and discussions

- Infer from multiple levels of analysis

- Segment social media activities and targets with appropriate business processes and technologies that optimize the listening and engagement opportunities

- Develop suites of internal/external/active/passive strategies and tactics designed to find the right listening and engagement combinations

- Pilot alternative listening/engagement opportunities, especially in areas that exploit the collaboration/connectivity strengths of social media, like crowdsourcing

- Identify the events, behaviors and conditions that qualify as real-time targets

- Build or buy a real-time listening/engagement capability

- Develop "what-if"/"if-then" scenarios for real-time listening/engagement

- Allocate SBI tasks along a man-machine continuum that realistically assigns the right tasks to the right agent

- Recognize – and invest in – a balanced man-machine SBI platform

- Continuously assess the state of SBI automation, especially as it pertains to vertical industry knowledge representation

- Define core competencies around technology generally and social media specifically

- Identify the specific social media capabilities necessary to deliver SBI

- Develop and implement a sourcing strategy that optimizes core competency assessments and SBI requirements

- Develop a comprehensive social media TCO model

- Develop an aligned (to business objectives and requirements) social media ROI model

- Distinguish between short-term and longer-term TCO and ROI metrics and adapt calculations to initial social media initiatives and longer-term continuous listening/engagement requirements as the social media channel inevitably becomes permanent

- Identify the business objectives and requirements wide and deep enough to support the development of a viable social media investment strategy
- Identify the questions whose answers constitute a strategy

- Adapt the strategy to investment results

Chapter 11 - Social Business Intelligence 2.0

SBI is off to a great start. But there are major changes in the works. In fact, there are at least five areas that will change how we think about SBI 2.0 over the next few years. The list includes:

- Big Data

- Real-Time Analytics

- Predictive Modeling

- Automation

- Governance

Big Data

If we don't solve the "big data" problem, we'll limit the problem-solving capacity of SBI. This is because the sheer volume of social data will overwhelm even today's most powerful listening/analysis/engagement tools – which are strained today from the growing number of tweets, blogs, posts and forums that deep (and real-time) social research requires for broad collection and analysis.

Wikipedia defines "big data" in a compelling – almost alarming – way:

> *"Big data consists of data sets that grow so large that they become awkward to work with using on-hand database management tools. Difficulties include capture, storage, search, sharing, analytics, and visualizing. This trend continues because of the benefits of working with larger and larger data sets allowing analysts to 'spot business trends, prevent diseases, combat crime.' Though a moving target, current limits are on the order of petabytes, exabytes and zettabytes of data. Scientists regularly encounter this problem in meteorology, genomics, connectomics, complex physics simulations, biological and environmental research, Internet search, finance and business informatics. Data sets also grow in size because they are in-*

creasingly being gathered by ubiquitous information-sensing mobile devices, aerial sensory technologies (remote sensing), software logs, cameras, microphones, Radio-frequency identification readers, and wireless sensor networks. The world's technological per capita capacity to store information has roughly doubled every 40 months since the 1980s (about every 3 years) and every day 2.5 quintillion bytes of data are created.

"One current feature of big data is the difficulty working with it using relational databases and desktop statistics/visualization packages, requiring instead 'massively parallel software running on tens, hundreds, or even thousands of servers.' The size of "big data" varies depending on the capabilities of the organization managing the set. 'For some organizations, facing hundreds of gigabytes of data for the first time may trigger a need to reconsider data management options. For others, it may take tens or hundreds of terabytes before data size becomes a significant consideration.'

"Examples include web logs; RFID; sensor networks; social networks; social data (due to the social data revolution), Internet text and documents; Internet search indexing; call detail records; astronomy, atmospheric science, genomics, biogeochemical, biological, and other complex and/or interdisciplinary scientific research; military surveillance; medical records; photography archives; video archives; and large-scale e-commerce."

But it's not just the volume of data that's undermining full SBI. There are technology issues as well:

"Big data requires exceptional technologies to efficiently process large quantities of data within tolerable elapsed times. Technologies being applied to big data include massively parallel processing (MPP) databases, data mining grids, distributed file systems, distributed databases, cloud computing platforms, the Internet, and scalable storage systems.

"Some but not all MPP relational databases have the ability to store and manage petabytes of data. Implicit is the ability to load, monitor, back-up, and optimize the use of the large data tables in the RDBMS.

"Real or near-real time information delivery is one of the defining characteristics of big data analytics. Latency is therefore avoided whenever and wherever possible. Data in memory is good. Data on spinning disk at the other end of a FC SAN connection is not. But perhaps worse than anything else, the cost of a SAN at the scale needed for analytics applications is thought to be prohibitive.

"There is a case to be made for shared storage in big data analytics. But storage vendors and the storage community in general have yet to make that case to big data analytics practitioners.

"Big data has emerged because we are living in a society which makes increasing use of data intensive technologies. There are 4.6 billion mobile-phone subscriptions worldwide and there are between 1 billion and 2 billion people accessing the internet. Basically, there are more people interacting with data or information than ever before. The world's effective capacity to exchange information through telecommunication networks was 281 petabytes in 1986, 471 petabytes in 1993, 2.2 exabytes in 2000, 65 exabytes in 2007 and it is predicted that the amount of traffic flowing over the internet will reach 667 exabytes annually by 2013."

Most of us have no idea what all of these numbers mean. But rest assured they are important – and daunting. If we're unable to collect, filter, classify, structure and analyze structured *and* unstructured data, we'll never be able to describe, explain and predict business behavior. New data architectures will be required to process big data – especially big unstructured data. *Hadoop* is a relatively new platform that enables big unstructured data processing. *Hadoop* was developed by Apache as an open source (free) platform, though a number of companies have built proprietary flavors of *Hadoop*, just as vendors built proprietary flavors on UNIX and Linux. The major database vendors – IBM, Microsoft and Oracle – are responding with their own enhanced platforms.

Some of the *Hadoop*-inspired proprietary products include (from Wikipedia):

- IBM offers InfoSphere BigInsights based on *Hadoop* in both a basic and enterprise edition.

- Zettaset offers new version of its Big Data Mgt Platform based on *Hadoop* Zettaset's Big Data Platform delivers High Availability via NameNode Failover.

- In May 2011, MapR Technologies, Inc. announced the availability of their distributed file system and MapReduce engine, the MapR Distribution for Apache *Hadoop*. The MapR product includes most Hadoop ecosystem components and adds capabilities such as snapshots, mirrors, NFS access and full read-write file semantics.

- Silicon Graphics International offers *Hadoop* optimized solutions based on the SGI Rackable and CloudRack server lines with implementation services.
- EMC released EMC Greenplum Community Edition and EMC Greenplum

- HD Enterprise Edition in May 2011.

- In June 2011, Yahoo! and Benchmark Capital formed Hortonworks Inc., whose focus is on making *Hadoop* more robust and easier to install, manage and use for enterprise users.

- Cloudera offers CDH (Cloudera's Distribution including Apache *Hadoop*) and Cloudera Enterprise.

- Google added AppEngine-MapReduce to support running *Hadoop* 0.20 programs on Google App Engine.

- In October 2011, Oracle announced the Big Data Appliance, which integrates *Hadoop*, Oracle Enterprise Linux, the R programming language, and a NoSQL database with the Exadata hardware.

- Dovestech has released Ocean Sync Hadoop Management Software Freeware Edition. The software allows users to control and monitor all aspects of an *Hadoop* cluster.

These products and services are the industry's first-line defense against the sheer volume of big data – not to mention the analytical requirements that extend from the voluminous new data sets.

The complexity of big data collection, filtering, structuring and analysis immediately suggests a sourcing analysis: should you develop your own big data capability or should you outsource it? As suggested in Chapter 10, unless big data base management is – or is expected to become – a core competency, you should leave big data filtering/structuring/analysis to the professionals.

Real-Time Analytics

What do you need to know *immediately*? What can wait? Real-time requirements are unique: there are not all that many events or conditions you need to know about immediately – but those that make the list are often especially threatening and impactful. When someone threatens a corporate executive in social media or shares information that could be harmful to individuals, groups or institutions, those responsible for reacting to information and threats need to know immediately.

"Real-time" means different things to different people. Even the definition of real-time changes across industries, companies and individuals. Wikipedia describes *real-time business intelligence (RTBI)* as:

> " ... *the process of delivering information about business operations as they occur. The speed of today's processing systems has moved classical data warehousing into the realm of real-time. The result is real-time business intelligence. Business transactions as they occur are fed to a real-time business intelligence system that maintains the current state of the enterprise. The RTBI system not only supports the classic strategic functions of data warehousing for deriving information and knowledge from past enterprise activity, but it also provides real-time tactical support to drive enterprise actions that react immediately to events as they occur. As such, it replaces both the classic data warehouse and the enterprise application integration (EAI) functions. Such event-driven processing is a basic tenet of real-time business intelligence.*

"In this context, real-time means a range from milliseconds to a few seconds after the business event has occurred. While traditional business intelligence presents historical data for manual analysis, real-time business intelligence compares current business events with historical patterns to detect problems or opportunities automatically. This automated analysis capability enables corrective actions to be initiated and/or business rules to be adjusted to optimize business processes.

"Real-time business intelligence makes sense for some applications but not for others – a fact that organizations need to take into account as they consider investments in real-time BI tools. The trick to deciding whether a real-time BI strategy would pay dividends is to understand your business needs and determine whether end users require immediate access to data for analytical purposes – or if something less than real time is fast enough."

The real issue around real-time is *latency*. According to Wikipedia:

"All real-time business intelligence systems have some latency, but the goal is to minimize the time from the business event happening to a corrective action or notification being initiated. Richard Hackathorn describes three types of latency:

- *Data latency; the time taken to collect and store the data*

- *Analysis latency; the time taken to analyze the data and turn it into actionable information*

- *Action latency; the time taken to react to the information and take action*

"Real-time business intelligence technologies are designed to reduce all three latencies to as close to zero as possible, whereas traditional business intelligence only seeks to reduce data latency and does not address analysis latency or action latency since both are governed by manual processes.

"Real-time Business Intelligence systems are event driven, and may use Event Stream Processing and Mashup (Web application hybrid) techniques to enable events to be analysed without being first transformed and stored in a database. These in-memory techniques have the

163

advantage that high rates of events can be monitored, and since data does not have to be written into databases data latency can be reduced to milliseconds."

Real-time is truly real-time when latency is extremely low. But database management vendors struggle with achieving even modest latency results. SBI 2.0 is a low latency world. Those that support SBI 2.0 must — and will — have substantial low-latency real-time collection / filtering / structuring / analysis capabilities.

The most capable SBI 2.0 vendors will have extremely low latency strategies that enable real-time and near-real-time processing. The vendors that actually achieve extremely low latency will have significant competitive advantage over those that don't. If real-time is one of your *bona fide* requirements, then make sure to vet the real-time capabilities of your vendor (or, possibly, your in-house team).

Predictive Modeling

Predictive modeling is a subset of predictive analytics, which is described by Wikipedia as encompassing:

" ... a variety of statistical techniques from modeling, machine learning, data mining and game theory that analyze current and historical facts to make predictions about future events. Predictive models exploit patterns found in historical and transactional data to identify risks and opportunities. Models capture relationships among many factors to allow assessment of risk or potential associated with a particular set of conditions, guiding decision making for candidate transactions.
"Predictive analytics is an area of statistical analysis that deals with extracting information from data and using it to predict future trends and behavior patterns. The core of predictive analytics relies on capturing relationships between explanatory variables and the predicted variables from past occurrences, and exploiting it to predict future outcomes. It is important to note, however, that the accuracy and usability of results will depend greatly on the level of data analysis and the quality of assumptions.

"Generally, the term predictive analytics is used to mean predictive modeling, 'scoring' data with predictive models, and forecasting. However, people are increasingly using the term to describe related analytical disciplines, such as descriptive modeling and decision modeling or optimization. These disciplines also involve rigorous data analysis, and are widely used in business for segmentation and decision making, but have different purposes and the statistical techniques underlying them vary.

"Predictive models analyze past performance to assess how likely a customer is to exhibit a specific behavior in the future in order to improve marketing effectiveness. This category also encompasses models that seek out subtle data patterns to answer questions about customer performance, such as fraud detection models. Predictive models often perform calculations during live transactions, for example, to evaluate the risk or opportunity of a given customer or transaction, in order to guide a decision. With advancement in computing speed, individual agent modeling systems can simulate human behavior or reaction to given stimuli or scenarios. The new term for animating data specifically linked to an individual in a simulated environment is avatar analytics.

"Descriptive models quantify relationships in data in a way that is often used to classify customers or prospects into groups. Unlike predictive models that focus on predicting a single customer behavior (such as credit risk), descriptive models identify many different relationships between customers or products. Descriptive models do not rank-order customers by their likelihood of taking a particular action the way predictive models do. Descriptive models can be used, for example, to categorize customers by their product preferences and life stage. Descriptive modeling tools can be utilized to develop further models that can simulate large number of individualized agents and make predictions.

"Predictive modeling is the process by which a model is created or chosen to try to best predict the probability of an outcome. In many cases the model is chosen on the basis of detection theory to try to guess the probability of an outcome given a set amount of input data, for example given an email determining how likely that it is spam.

"Predictive modeling is used extensively in analytical customer relationship management and data mining to produce customer-level models that describe the likelihood that a customer will take a particular action. The actions are usually sales, marketing and customer retention related.

"For example, a large consumer organization such as a mobile telecommunications operator will have a set of predictive models for product cross-sell, product deep-sell and churn. It is also now more common for such an organization to have a model of savability using an uplift model. This predicts the likelihood that a customer can be saved at the end of a contract period (the change in churn probability) as opposed to the standard churn prediction model."

As discussed in Chapter 10, social media can be modeled to solve a variety of descriptive, explanatory and predictive problems. It's important to think about social media modeling as exploratory. There are relationships among business events and conditions that we currently cannot see and do not understand. They are therefore unpredictable. What's the relationship between "complaining" and customer loyalty? Obvious? Or are there counter-intuitive elements of the relationships where complaining predicts to even *greater* loyalty and sales?

What about the relationship among social rants and sales, revenue and profitability? What happens when competitors praise each other? The structured modeling of social behavior requires hypotheses, data and deep domain expertise. Structured modeling is focused on validating hypotheses about consumer, supplier and employee behavior. Insight from subject matter experts informs the hypotheses generation process that ultimately confirms or disconfirms assumptions and expectations about what social data reveals. Structured social modeling is no different from the structured modeling or other structured or unstructured data. Companies have been slicing and dicing data for decades. The whole field of business intelligence/data-mining/analytics was born from the desire to describe, explain and predict behavior.

The unstructured modeling of social behavior also requires hypotheses and data – but "barefoot empiricism" as well, where hypotheses are open-ended. "Discovery" here can be random: "let's see what correlates to what." Much of this discovery can be automated in which patterns are searched 24/7.

Automation

Another important technology that will affect SBI 2.0 is automation fueled by increasingly intelligent embedded and special-purpose artificial intelligence (AI)-enabled applications.

Analysts love to talk about the resurgence of "AI" about once every five years or so. The fact is that AI has never gone away. When something (someone?) like Watson appears from IBM and beats Ken Jennings on *Jeopardy* everyone takes notice and declares yet another return from the technology dead for AI and all of its cousins.

Some of you may remember AI as the darling emerging technology of the 1970s and 1980s. A ton of money was thrown at the field and countless doctoral dissertations were written by budding knowledge engineers, expert systems developers, and natural language parsers.

The US Department of Defense (DOD) led the pack with money, hype and a variety of applications that turned out to be more prototypical than real. Nevertheless, decades later we're still finding new applications for AI and all of the major (and not-so-major) technology companies have embedded "intelligence" into their applications.

AI is an interdisciplinary sub-field of systems engineering, psychology, electrical engineering and computer science that seeks to recreate in computer software the processes by which humans solve problems. AI "knowledge engineers" extract expertise from professionals like doctors, geologists and signal processors, and then structure it in a way that permits relatively flexible problem-solving in a specific area, such as medical diagnosis, geological drilling or data analysis.

AI systems differ from conventional ones in a number of important ways. First, conventional systems store and manipulate data within some very specific processing boundaries. AI systems store and apply knowledge to a variety of unspecified problems within selected problem domains. Conventional systems are passive, whereas AI systems actively interact with – and adapt to – their users. Conventional systems cannot infer beyond certain pre-programmed limits, but AI systems can make inferences, implement rules of thumb and solve problems in much the same way we routinely decide whether or not to buy a Ford or a Chevy, or accept a new professional challenge.

The representation of knowledge is the mainstay of AI, expert systems and intelligent systems technology research and development. If knowledge and expertise can be captured in computer software and applied at a moment's notice, then major breakthroughs may be possible in the production and distribution of knowledge – and in the execution of transactions. If it's possible to capture the best medical diagnosticians, the best managers, the best intelligence analysts, and the best customer service representatives in a set of flexible and friendly computer-based systems, then productivity and efficiency will explode (as rapidly as costs decline).

Conventional and special purpose software languages permit intelligent systems designers to represent knowledge in several ways. The most widely utilized knowledge representation technique involves the development of cognitive rules of thumb usually expressed in "if ... form." In the world of high finance, for example, it's very easy to imagine a rule-based investment advisory system containing a rule like, "if gold falls below \$1,000 per ounce, then invest 25% of available resources in gold." A system with a thousand such rules might prove very efficient since it could continually monitor investment conditions around the world and, via its rules, allocate resources accordingly.

As you've no doubt already surmised, the key to the power of all rule-based systems lies in the accuracy and depth of their rules. Bad rules produce bad conclusions, just as bad human probability estimates frequently result in bad outcomes. It's the job of the knowledge engineer to make sure that the rules represent substantive expertise to the fullest extent possible. This requirement, in turn, means that rule-based systems can never stop developing. In order for them to keep pace with the field they're trying to represent electronically, they must routinely be fed new rules.

As suggested above, one of the earliest AI research goals was to develop computer-based systems that could understand free-form language. The "natural language processing" branch of AI represents knowledge by endowing software with the capability to understand the meaning of words, phrases, parts of speech and concepts that are expressed textually in English, French, German or whatever language is "natural" to the intended user. It's now possible to converse directly with tablets and smart phones in the same way we converse with human colleagues.

Some things to consider about AI:

- Complex processes that have resisted conventional systems and analysis procedures can sometimes be addressed by intelligent systems technology, especially complex real-time data integration and mining problems, problems that require immediate action-reaction, and really tough problems due primarily to the sheer volume of data or the size of decision spaces.

- Automation is now possible in selected areas and will become more possible in additional domains. We know, for example, that it's possible to automate marketing campaigns and many companies are using various levels of embedded intelligence to do just that.

- AI, expert systems and intelligent systems technology may well generate huge returns on investments – and provide a technology-based response to increasing competition, the volatility of business models and the pace of technology change.

- Increasingly, instead of developing whole new systems, we will be asked to improve existing systems. There is enormous leverage in the re-engineering of existing systems via the insertion of expert systems and other intelligent systems technology.

- There are myriad functions, tasks and sub-tasks that can be addressed via intelligent systems technology inherently more efficient than conventional computational technologies.

- Intelligent systems are morphing into "intelligent agents."

Chances are you're already using a variety of pretty sophisticated intelligent tools and techniques – embedded in a variety of applications on your laptops/tablets, in your servers and via the Web. We're suggesting that another wave of intelligent applications that will revolutionize how you compute and communicate: intelligent *SBI*. Intelligent systems will help social media collection through learning, filtering and structuring through adaptive templates and modeling via automated hypothesis generation and testing. In fact, AI will have a profound impact on all aspects of data organization, structure, search and retrieval. "Intelligent agents" will support SBI that performs routine tasks, information overload reduction, collaboration, group problem-solving, network and systems management, planning, negotiating and sharing, among countless other activities and functions. SBI will be directly enhanced by AI and the automation it enables.

Governance

Who should "own" SBI?　What should SBI governance look like?

These are huge questions, since every new initiative in every company on the planet requires a strategy, advocates and objectives – as it struggles to identify and power among enemies dedicated to defunding and undermining the new initiative's birth, growth and maturity. We've seen all this before. Remember the religious wars about where the first Web sites should sit organizationally, administratively and "politically"? Corporate "IT" believed it should own the Web sites. Marketing believed it should own them, and the business units felt that *their* web sites should be owned by *them*! Of course. SBI is another debate. Where should it sit? Who should control it? How should SBI be defined and leveraged?

Technology governance – like all corporate governance – is about decision rights ideally organized in "RACI" (responsible/accountable/consultative/informed) playbooks that describe who's allowed to acquire, deploy and support business technology. In fully centralized technology organizations, all of the decision rights belong to the centralized control group; in decentralized organizations, decision rights are diffuse; and in federated technology organizations, rights are shared. Companies must decide what works for their industry, leadership and corporate culture. But without clear, consistent technology governance, companies will – at great risk – under-invest or over-invest in digital technology – and this definitely includes SBI.

If companies fail to define and implement the right SBI governance model, they will fail because they will be unable to discover or exploit SBI technology, unable to adapt quickly to national and global challenges and, perhaps most importantly, unable to evolve new SBI technology-enabled business models and processes (like the ones discussed above). While new technologies are all around us, unless there's a plan to optimize their acquisition, deployment and support they will barely impact corporate strategies or tactics. Technology governance is the essential enabler here. Not technology strategies – which can be developed and codified – but never implemented. Not corporate strategies – which *assume* technology – but seldom if ever detail technology investments. Technology governance clarifies what should be purchased, how technologies should be deployed and who should manage – *"own"* – the technology acquisition, deployment and support process. The empowerment aspect of governance is what unleashes technology's contribution to growth and profitability. If managers and executives can make the right technology investments at the right time – without the constraint of rigid governance structures and processes – technology's contribution to the business can be wide and deep.

The concept of "participatory governance" is a response to the relatively closed governance structures and processes so prevalent in the 20th and early 21st centuries. The concept of participatory governance emerged after extensive work – interviews and surveys – with business technology managers and executives.

For decades, IT governance has been about centralization, standardization and control – the essence of old school governance. IT communicated to its business partners the limits of technology, that tech-technology-was-a-cost center and technology's security vulnerabilities – all designed to keep the control of technology in the hands of a few well inside the corporate firewall. Companies invested in this perspective to the point where business executives saw technology as an inhibitor, not an enabler. There are still a lot of business-technology adversarial relationships out there anchored in this perspective – fed by years of nurturing – that sees technology as a necessary evil – not a source of cost-effective business enablement or a bona fide business partner. Perhaps surprisingly, technology managers are often the first to sound the alarm, warning that new technologies are unproven, not secure and expensive – and therefore best left in the hands of those who understand it. This argument for old-style control is just that, a 20th century appeal for the return to centralized control of technology assets.

Technology itself is decentralizing. "End-users" are not just the passive recipients of digital technology but pro-active adopters and even creators of technology. When did all this begin? Probably in the late 1980s when first generation client-server computing emerged, which distributed computing power across the enterprise. When the Internet became a transaction platform the world changed forever, and when the industry gave us integration and interoperability standards it was anyone's game. SBI is no different: it's "available" from many vendors via cloud delivery. Corporate IT often doesn't even know that business units have procured SBI from third-party providers.

Renting (versus buying and installing) software calls for new governance models. Vendor management will emerge as a core competency for many companies. Service level agreements (SLAs) must be managed for performance; business units and central IT both have roles to play here. Similarly, renting hardware through cloud delivery will emerge as a viable alternative to building and maintaining huge server farms. This trend will challenge governance as well, requiring cooperation between business and technology units since "control" will now involve a third party – the cloud provider – committed to providing support to the whole company, not just central IT.

Consumerization has changed the way we introduce technology. Technology adoption actually occurs before employees enter the building. Web 2.0 and social media technologies (wikis, blogs, podcasts, RSS filters, virtual worlds, crowdsourcing, mashups, folksonomies and social networks) are making their way into companies at an incredible pace. Who's controlling this process? Corporate IT departments are struggling to keep up with the use of these tools by employees, customers and suppliers. Mashups are the creation of pieces spread out all over the place, that is, inside and outside the corporate firewall. Who controls the applications programming interfaces (APIs), the components and widgets that mash into new applications? How do you prevent blogs and wikis from springing up on an employee's laptop?

Web-based applications represent a challenge to old governance models. They are deployed almost instantly. Changes to existing transaction-oriented Web sites are immediate. Who governs all this?

All of this calls for new organizational structures. "Headquarters" needs to decentralize. Standards need to become architectural and procedural, not based on brands, models or vendors. CIOs and CTOs need to focus on infrastructure optimization, alternative technology delivery models, architecture and not much else. The business needs to focus on requirements, application development (within architectural standards) and the deployment of fast/cheap technologies like Web 2.0 and social media technologies. If companies don't adjust their governance then the business technology partnership will collapse. There will be major push-back from the businesses that want to move quickly, cheaply and adaptively. If central IT organizations provide roadblocks to these operating principles, they will end-run the organizations.

Technology governance is something every company needs. But it's also something that most companies would prefer not to discuss – or publish. But without explicit, consistent, well-communicated and well-supported governance, companies will experience some degree of chaos in the technology acquisition, deployment and support process. Participatory governance stakeholders include all corporate clients, business unit clients, vendors, partners and cloud-based participants. Corporate clients are the mainstay. They use SBI technology to communicate, collaborate, solve problems, make decisions, retrieve data and all of the other operational tasks that define their professional existence. Business unit clients see technology as a conduit to their customers, suppliers, alliance partners and colleagues in the cloud. Vendors, service providers, partners and colleagues in the cloud are also governance stakeholders. Vendors and service providers are special stakeholders since the products and services they offer define de facto governance. Companies that outsource huge amounts of their operational infrastructures knowingly (or unwittingly) outsource their technology standards and the governance around those standards. While the standards themselves can be broad (a break from the past's interpretation of "standards"), they nonetheless define what the hardware, software and service offerings will be. Environments that outsource lots of technology and technology services share governance with their providers. Similarly, suppliers and other partners frequently require specific technology-based transaction processing which also results in shared governance.

Participatory governance acknowledges the expansion of the number of governance stakeholders, the commoditization of technology, consumerization and the increased practice of outsourcing operational and – increasingly – strategic technology. It is impossible to ignore these trends and continue to see governance through a 20th century lens.

The argument here is to explicitly acknowledge the trends and to adjust governance to accommodate the stakeholders who all see their objectives differently. Sharing governance authority is a natural result of how the world itself is changing. It's impossible for IT executives to expect to exercise the kind of control they exercised in the 1980s or 1990s. The new business technology alignment opportunity is through participatory governance – which will dramatically accelerate the adoption of SBI processes and technologies.

Big data collection, filtering, structuring and analysis, real-time analytics, predictive modeling and automation all require governance – and governance impacts SBI. It's important to define SBI governance collaboratively to include the right stakeholders.

Part IV

Business Intelligence Is Forever Social

Chapter 12 - Business Intelligence-to-Social Business Intelligence

We've just scratched the surface of social media and SBI. As the number of posts, blogs and tweets continues to rise, the number of sites increases and mobility grows, there's no question that the volume and focus of social medial data, information and knowledge will dramatically expand. "Big data" problems aside, the volume and focus will permit analyses that we've dreamed about conducting for decades.

Social media companies will be able to perform lexical, semantic and statistical analysis of unstructured data, they will be able to filter out noise, understand good data deeper, and integrate more relevant actionable data to more functions and systems across the enterprise. Analytical models will emerge that will instantly and continuously measure sentiment, consumer behavior and second/ third/fourth-order correlations among products, services, sentiment and consumer behavior.

Social business intelligence will morph into social intelligence where social media data, information and knowledge is leveraged across personal, professional, business, government and non-governmental organization behavior. It will become a mainstream channel that's measured in real-time through analytical models that describe, explain, predict and prescribe behavior. You need to focus on social media opportunities, risks and strategies to exploit this important new 24/7 channel.

The promise of BI has turned the performance corner. While we're still cleaning, migrating and securing data, and worrying about platform compatibility, we've also connected BI to business performance management, a step that reflects rising expectations about what the BI end-game looks like. We've begun the journey toward structured/unstructured data integration/interpretation and real-time analytics – and also semantic processing, anticipating Web 3.0 and SBI 2.0. Almost all of the major BI players have found new homes. All systems are go. BI – *& SBI* – 2.0 are real – and ready.

Storage and analysis capabilities map on to a pretty standard under-standing of database management, but there are some major differ-ences between how this will unfold compared with how software envi-environments were configured a decade or so ago. First and foremost, we're talking about the integration of functionality and platforms through increasingly open interoperability standards – in spite of how mixed the emotions might be across the proprietary software vendors. This is clearly different. Secondly, BI is now linked with problem-solving-driven business performance management, which also makes sense given that BI 2.0 and SBI 2.0 are really about cockpit-like busi-ness process optimization. This is also different from the 1990s. The range of new technologies that makes BI/SBI 2.0 possible is wide and deep: there are robust new hardware architectures, whole new soft-ware delivery models, and integration capabilities that are part proprie-tary and part open. This is all different from where the "database management" world was in the 1980s and 1990s. Social media, the source of increasing amounts of unstructured user-generated data, in-formation and knowledge that must be gathered, stored and analyzed, *represents a natural extension of BI.*

Data/information/knowledge storage is also changing via commoditi-zation on the one hand and consumerization on the other. The mon-ster database management systems (DBMSs) of the past are quickly morphing into flexible relational/ object-oriented repositories capable of retrieving and integrating data from all sorts of sources. On the consumer end are Web-based platforms that enable tagging, book-marking and content management. Many of these tools are "free" or nearly free, suggesting that open source software (OSS) has signifi-cantly penetrated data/information/knowledge storage, analysis and problem-solving (Sun Microsystems paid $1B for MySQL – and then was purchased by Oracle). More importantly, the way we think about "data base management" is changing, as DBMS capabilities extend well beyond the corporate firewall. The discussion of *Hadoop* in Chap-ter 10 focused on the power and availability of alternative data base management and BI technologies. Clearly, *Hadoop* represents a differ-ent way to think about data base management.

Analysis assumes the integration and interpretation of all sources of data, information and knowledge including especially structured *and* unstructured data/ information/knowledge. The impact of social media on data/information/knowledge creation is enormous: no one accurately calculated the amount of data that social media applications would generate (largely because we all underestimated the volume of user-generated data/information/knowledge). Will the volume of unstructured data/information/knowledge eventually overtake structured data/ information/knowledge? Yes. Everyone is now focused on gathering, storing and analyzing data/information/knowledge generated by social media applications. The integration of structured and unstructured data/information/knowledge – and the inferences possible from that integration – is where the action will be in the coming years.

But the end-game is really about real-time analytics and the problem-solving it enables.

Multi- and many-core hardware architectures are making it possible to collect, store and analyze data almost as fast as it's found. Data integration technology has also improved to the point where the source, nature and format of data hardly matters. Predictive analytics is the new Holy Grail. Real-time analysis is the enabling goal.

All this is about problem-solving in real-time. The cockpit metaphor is still a good one: every manager and executive aspires to business "combat" in a high performance vehicle controlled by a real-time transactional dashboard that enables immediate, targeted decision-making of all kinds and at all levels of the organization.

We're in the final stages of the conceptual phase of true BI as we transition to applications and processes that solve important business problems. Of course there are significant software applications that enable all sorts of data analyses of manufacturing, customer relationships, products and transaction processes. Of course there are major data base management vendors that provide embedded and reasonably integrated data analysis tools, and there are definitely companies that run parts of their business from descriptive analytical portals that provide insight into their operations. But there are some major problems connected with achieving nirvana. There are still huge issues around the quality, location and integration of data/information/knowledge. Companies still have to invest heavily in their data infrastructures and architectures to exploit BI opportunities. This investment significantly reduces the return on BI investments and sometimes even challenges the overall cost-benefit of BI. When "benefits realization" gets muddled in the executive suite – or worse, in the board of directors – technology investments become vulnerable. How many BI projects have failed over the past ten years? Like CRM applications, BI projects have often met with resistance, have frequently cost far more than expected and have too frequently failed to generate any significant business impact. Is this because BI technology is bad? It's much more likely that the immaturity of our data environments is at the root of BI "failures" than the inherent weakness of either the BI concept or generally available BI tools.

The real impact of BI is therefore dependent upon several maturing streams of innovation and management. Let's first describe what the perfect picture looks like in 2015. By that time many business transactions will be largely automated with a variety of if-then triggers throughout operations. Information will not be inspected by humans as much as it's assessed by software. Business rules will drive most business processes – rules that are manually changed but much more frequently triggered by the same if-then rules that will together automate key processes and transactions. The more data, information and knowledge brought to bear on operations and transaction processing the closer we all get to real-time optimization, the ultimate objective of dynamic strategy and tactics. When companies know exactly what's happening with their customers, manufacturing processes and suppliers in real-time, when the same companies have elaborate rules engines at work, and when these companies automate the rules, we'll have dynamic real-time optimization, the ultimate expression of BI 2.0. BI matures when there's real-time insight into what's happening, embedded judgments (rules) about what's good and bad about what's happening, and the automated and quasi-automated ability to do something about what's happening.

The intersection of these distinct disciplines – BI, predictive analytics and real-time processing – defines BI – *and enables SBI.*

Chapter 13 - Conclusions

We've covered a lot of ground in this book. We began with an analysis of the social media and SBI landscape. We then presented some cases in the application of SBI. We looked at what's coming down the road for both BI and SBI. We also provided a due diligence checklist for selecting an SBI partner.

Social business intelligence has – in just a few short years – become a major driver of operational and strategic decisions that cross-cut corporate awareness, brands, customer service, product development, reputation management and, ultimately, business purpose. Social media impacts the top and bottom lines of all companies that sell and service anything. Just three years ago "social business intelligence" was an unknown and undefined capability; companies that ignore social media today are at competitive risk. The decade of the customer has been proclaimed – and there's every indication that direct customer (employee, supplier) power will persist forever. Social media is a communications and collaboration channel that is widening and deepening every day. In fact, we're still learning how to use the growing streams of social media data. Analytics will be redefined by social media as we perfect the means by which structured and unstructured data, information and knowledge is collected, filtered, structured, modeled and analyzed. Real-time will replace old-time. The crowd will replace focus groups. Insight will replace guesswork.

We've only just begun: imagine what will happen when the Zippies are in charge.

About the Authors

Stephen J. Andriole is the Thomas G. Labrecque Professor of Business Technology at Villanova University where he teaches and directs applied research in business technology management. He is also a Fellow at the Cutter Consortium. He is formerly a Professor of Information Systems & Electrical & Computer Engineering at Drexel University and the George Mason Institute Professor and Chairman of the Department of Information Systems & Systems Engineering at George Mason University. Stephen J. Andriole was the Director of the Cybernetics Technology Office of the Defense Advanced Research Projects Agency (DARPA). He was also the Chief Technology Officer and Senior Vice President of Safeguard Scientifics, Inc. and the Chief Technology Officer and Senior Vice President for Technology Strategy at CIGNA Corporation.

Some of his thirty books include *Interactive Computer-Based Systems Design & Development* (Petrocelli Books, Inc., 1983), *Microcomputer Decision Support Systems* (QED Information Sciences, Inc., 1985), *Applications in Artificial Intelligence* (Petrocelli Books, Inc., 1986), *Information System Design Principles for the 90s* (AFCEA International Press, 1990), the *Sourcebook of Applied Artificial Intelligence* (McGraw-Hill, 1992), a (co-authored with Len Adelman) book on user interface technology for Lawrence Erlbaum Associates, Inc. entitled *Cognitive Systems Engineering* (1995), a book for McGraw-Hill entitled *Managing Systems Requirements: Methods, Tools & Cases* (1996), books on the *2nd Digital Revolution* (2005) and *Technology Due Diligence* (2009) – for IGI Press – and *Best Practices in Business Technology Management* (2009) and *IT's All About the People* (2011) for Auerbach Publications. He has published articles in the *Cutter IT Journal, Software Development, IEEE Software*, the *Communications of the ACM*, the *Communications of the AIS, IEEE IT Professional* and the *Journal of Information Technology Research*, among other journals. His *IT's All About the People* won the #4 spot for Best Business Technology Books in 2011 by CIO Insight Magazine.

Mark D. Langsfeld is an expert in social media and business intelligence. He advises large enterprises on how to manage risk, engage with customers and drive innovation. He is the Co-Founder and Chief Strategy Officer of AKUDA LABS and ListenLogic.

AKUDA LABS (akuda.com) is revolutionizing real-time, streaming big data filtering, classification and analytics. Its proprietary Pulsar hypercomputing platform is the fastest, most efficient real-time streaming classification engine available, processing 500 million streaming classification operations per second (SCOPS) on a path to 1+ billion SCOPS.

ListenLogic (ListenLogic.com) is the leading streaming big data business intelligence provider delivering companies real-time monitoring of risks and opportunities and deep inspection of markets and products out of social media chaos. ListenLogic serves as an ongoing proof point for Pulsar's incredible hypercomputing technology.

Previously, he was the Co-Founder of Mediagistics, a search analytics and arbitrage company. Prior to that he served as Vice President of New Products at Move, Inc. He was also Vice President of Product Strategy for 4anything.com. He was also a Financial Analyst at BT Alex Brown in the Real Estate Investment Banking Group.

Mark R. Harrington is an accomplished, versatile marketer, Mark's unique expertise spans publishing to payments and education to ecommerce. He's excelled in Inc 500s to Fortune 500s and been instrumental in landmark exits worth over a half billion dollars, helping catapult an array of pioneering industry solutions. He is CMO of AKUDA LABS and ListenLogic.

As Client Delivery Head on Citi Prepaid's Management Team he led Marketing, Design, Implementation and Client Services for clients like Apple, BMW, Disney, Google, P&G and Verizon. He helped drive revenue 36x, sat on Citi's Global Marketing Council and Social Media Committee and was GM for Ecount's $220MM Citi acquisition, receiving the Bertie-Bob Leadership Award.

As Half.com's co-founder and youngest Management Team member, he ran Retention Marketing, managing 75% of gross merchandise sales. Acquired by eBay for $350MM, Half hit profitability largely due to his pioneering of the P2P textbook market, earning him eBay's Out of This World Award. He also helped devise "one of the greatest publicity coups in history" (*Time Magazine*) Half.com, Oregon.

At Infonautics he co-founded Company Sleuth (*PC Magazine* Top 100) and Sports Sleuth (Yahoo! Top 50), earning him their Innovation Award. At Pearson he promoted four national Top 10 higher ed titles earning him their Summit Award.

He holds a BS in Marketing, Honors with Distinction, from The Pennsylvania State University Smeal College of Business and was a Melbourne Wesley Cummings and Dorothy M. Kelly Scholar.

Vincent J. Schiavone is the Co-Founder, Chairman and CEO of AKUDA LABS (akuda.com) and ListenLogic (ListenLogic.com), a pioneering "Social Business Intelligence" provider that delivers leading corporations with powerful insight from the rapidly expanding universe of customer comment and interaction to effectively understand and manage risk, reputation and customer engagement.

At the heart of ListenLogic is AKUDA LABS, a deep research and development team assembled from leading developers and experts from the public, private and academic sectors. AKUDA LABS is the developer of the state-of-the-art Pulsar Social Big Data Analytics Platform. Its extreme stream-data flow architecture gives companies the capability to collect, filter, structure and analyze social (and structured) data in real-time with upwards of an industry-leading one billion classified operations per second.

An entrepreneur, investor and author, Mr. Schiavone has created and grown a number of firms, driven by his commitment to helping create a platform for trust in the digital economy. Each of his companies has focused on one of the three elements: privacy, security and performance.

Mr. Schiavone focused first on privacy when he founded ePrivacy Group, a privacy consulting company and trusted email technology incubator. ePrivacy Group developed the framework and technology for a set of services like the Trusted Sender program, TEOS (a Trusted Email Open Standard), and SpamSquelcher.

This work led to the launch of TurnTide, an enterprise anti-spam technology company that was ultimately acquired by Symantec.

Security was the industry targeted by InfoSec Labs, a boutique consulting and training company serving global 2000 clients. InfoSec Labs was an early player in the security space providing assessments, penetration testing and strategy for its clients. InfoSec Labs pioneered practices still in use today and was acquired by SafeNet (SFNT).

In addition to his role at ListenLogic, Mr. Schiavone is a managing partner in the Acentio Group (acentio.com) which offers guidance on the optimization of business technology in medium-to-large sized enterprises, a senior consultant with Cutter Consortium (cutter.com), a strategic IT research and advisory firm and a managing partner at the investment firm Prioratus, LLC (prioratus.com).

Luis F. Stevens, Co-founder and Chief Technology Officer of AKUDA LABS (akuda.com) and ListenLogic (ListenLogic.com), is an expert in super-computing, data modeling, and semantic analysis. He holds nine US patents and has served strategic technology leadership roles with several of the leading technology organizations, including Silicon Graphics, Intel and IBM. He's also developed landmark technology systems for organizations like the NSA, NASA and Los Alamos National Laboratory.

Under Mr. Stevens' leadership, AKUDA LABS is revolutionizing real-time, streaming big data filtering, classification and analytics. Its proprietary hypercomputing platform is the fastest, most efficient real-time streaming classification engine available, processing 500 million streaming classification operations per second (SCOPS) on a path to 1+ billion SCOPS.

Previously, Luis was the Founder and Chief Technology Officer of Knogee, a semantic search engine company. Prior to this, he served as Chief Architect at Cast Iron Systems (acquired by IBM), where he led the design and development of an application integration appliance.

As Chief Software Architect at NetBoost (acquired by Intel), he led the development of system software and compilers for a multi-engine network processor. He went on to serve as Principal Architect for Intel after NetBoost's acquisition.

He was the Lead Architect at SGI where he led the development of the ORIGIN NUMA Multiprocessor System, which was largely based on his research at Stanford University and is still in use by the NSA. He is a graduate of Stanford University.